Advice for the Lovelorn Pakistani

Advice *for the* Lovelorn Pakistani

Paula Evans

MOHAVE PUBLISHING
LAS VEGAS, NEVADA

This is a work of creative nonfiction. Some parts, including names and identifying details of people, have been fictionalized.

Copyright © 2020 Paula Evans

All rights reserved. No part of this publication may be reproduced, distributed, or transmitted in any form or by any means, including photocopying, recording, or other electronic or mechanical methods, without the prior written permission of the publisher, except in the case of brief quotations embodied in critical reviews and certain other noncommercial uses permitted by copyright law. For permission requests, write to the publisher, addressed "Attention: Permissions Coordinator," at the address below.

Mohave Publishing LLC
8635 West Sahara Avenue, Unit 4012
Las Vegas, Nevada 89117

Printed in the United States of America

First Printing 2020

ISBN 978-0-9979857-3-3
ebook **ISBN** 978-0-9979857-4-0
Library of Congress Control Number: 2020908088

www.mohavepublishing.com

Cover designed with resources from Freepik.com

For Evelyn

Acknowledgements

Anyone who teaches anything anywhere to anybody will have amusing stories about students, assignments, and life in general. Are they exaggerations? Yes and no. Truth is stranger than fiction but sometimes it is hard to tell the difference. And the more outrageous a situation the funnier it becomes.

So while the characters and situations are based on "kernels of truth," this is a work of fiction. I came up with the title first and then had to write a story to fit. I truly do not intend to offend anyone or disparage any culture, ethnicity, or religion. This is a humorous look at life from one limited point of view, with a lot of "Wouldn't it be funny if . . ." thrown in for good measure.

But what isn't fiction is the deep gratitude I owe to Dane Ronnow of Mohave Publishing. His lovely wife, Dianne, is a college friend of mine and she persuaded Dane to take a chance. Dianne found the right cover photo based on the design concept of artist Jennifer Stevens. I am eternally grateful to all for their assistance.

I do also thank Greg Keehn and Ryan Stinchcomb whom I met in 2016 through the Northwest Indiana Writing Project. My "buddy" Jenaffer Beasley just happened to pop into my classroom with the information about this program (after the registration deadline). Miraculously we were both accepted, and part of the four-week seminar was an opportunity to share something we were working on. Ryan and Greg were my "Guinea pigs" and they actually liked the premise and offered me insight and encouragement. We only got to share twice, but I do appreciate the support from these two gentlemen.

Advice for the Lovelorn Pakistani

Chapter 1

I'm not sure how I ended up being the go-to person for marital advice. I've never been married. I've never even had a boyfriend. I didn't grow up in a two-parent family. Was it listening so much to all those harpies at the weekly Saturday night Bingo games that "educated" me? Was it watching too much TV growing up? Or was it just common sense?

I'm from the Midwest. My name is Jane Smith. You can't get much plainer than that.

People often asked me why I never married. It just never happened. How does it "never" happen? I don't know—it just didn't. No, I didn't meet guys. I also wasn't looking. Everything else in my life just happened—why didn't this?

I could never understand women, even though I'm one of them. They would carry on that they just *had* to be married, but once they *were* married, they couldn't say a nice thing about their husbands. The husbands were stupid in every sense of the word.

So why did you marry them? I never directly asked them, but I sure thought about it. *Why pledge yourself to someone you don't even like?* I didn't understand that.

Paula Evans

I did ask this question, once, at work. I was an adjunct professor at a local university. It was a satellite campus of Central Heights University. I was teaching English Composition. The others were teaching English Literature, math, and Spanish. It was an eclectic group, which made it more interesting than it sounded.

Between classes we adjuncts shared an office, with several desks and a handful of computers. It was cozy enough—most of us didn't spend that much time there. With luck, our classes were back to back and we could come in time for class and leave immediately afterward. We were obligated to have "office hours" in case a student wanted to talk about their grade. But with the proliferation of computers, most things were handled electronically. Between classes we would gather in the office and compare stories of who had the dumbest students.

There were five of us, three females and two males, just talking and somehow the topic turned to marriage and the reason "why bother." Erin, the married woman, simply smiled at Michelle and me, both of us single. The two men were a different story. One was thrice divorced. I figured the topic and the audience was safe enough, so I broached the subject. "Why do women insist on getting married when the guy is too stupid to start with?"

The other man, Frank, slowly wheeled back his office chair. He was in his late fifties as far as we could tell—men don't age the same way women do. He had graying hair and was balding, so it was a safe guess he was that old. He wasn't going to get in the crossfire. He was very tight-lipped about his private life. This was the first time any of us knew anything about Frank—

like if he was married or not. He didn't wear a wedding ring. But he did have the sense to back away from controversy. His wife taught him well, or his mother did. Who knows?

Erin's smile was plastered across her face. She was in her very early thirties and had been married about five years. Their son just turned two. She was the first to reply to my query. "Well, I can't speak for others, but it works for us because we work opposite shifts and we never see each other."

That was true—her husband worked a night shift at a local factory, she taught during the day. No need for childcare this way.

John, the divorced man, began to drawl. "Weeellll, let me tell you."

We women all smiled at each other—this was going to be good. With three failed marriages, we surely didn't expect him to be a fount of advice. Or maybe he could be—he could tell us what doesn't work.

And he did.

"The problem is women don't want to be talked down to. They want to be talked *to*. That's why I have so many female friends online in chat rooms. They want a conversation with someone who isn't going to judge them. They have ideas and want to converse with someone—anyone!"

That makes sense. It's a basic human need, isn't it? The need to be loved, the need to matter to someone. But that still didn't explain how I became the Miss Know-it-All-of-Marital-Advice to my married students. This was how I got all of my information—bull sessions at work. And television, of course. Because we all know how realistic *that* is.

Little did I know this little discussion would be the impetus for Frank to test my skills.

I'm not sure why I became a teacher. This thought of career did cross my mind from time to time. One of the few pieces of advice my mother gave me (few as in it had some merit, as opposed to most other things she said) was to get that teaching license. I loved to play school when I was little with my sister, who was ten years older and already in high school. It wasn't that often and she wasn't the model student (because she was always talking to the "other students" in class while I was teaching. Mind you, there were only two of us in the room.) When it was her turn to teach and my turn to be the student, she wouldn't call on me. And people wonder why I have an inferiority complex?

I was teaching a few college courses during the day at Central Heights University. It was one of the top schools in the nation and I was at one of the satellite campuses out in the middle of nowhere, it seemed. Imagine watching *The Wizard of Oz*, when the characters all see the Emerald City in the distance, surrounded by the poppy field. This was that place, except substitute corn for poppies. But it was also the butt of more than a few jokes. Often referred to by its initials, CHU (pronounced chew, or choo), its mascot was a choo-choo—I mean train. Pity the poor engineering students . . . What type of engineer do you want to be? Are you majoring in Mechanical? Civil? Electrical? Diesel? Coal?

Advice For The Lovelorn Pakistani

As far as jobs go, this was a good one—few hours inside the classroom, but plenty outside of it grading papers. I did enjoy it. I love the atmosphere of a college campus. There is nothing like it anywhere. It's a proving ground for young people, an incubator of maturity. On the plus side, it really improved my copy-editing skills—I rented myself out during my own college years for the foreign students on campus. So consequently, my poor CHU students didn't stand a chance. But, damn, by the time I was done with them they were good writers.

Hmm. I was editing papers for foreign students . . . and I still am. I detect a trend. But I digress.

My first semester at CHU might have been the formative one for this trend. It was my first teaching job, as an adjunct professor of English composition (the requisite freshman writing class). There was a method to the madness which took me a while to pick up on, but it was a great introduction to teaching. I had two classes that semester, both fifty minutes long, which met three days a week. Just long enough to not freak me out, and short enough that I didn't have to try to entertain. That was the nice thing about teaching college—you didn't have to entertain and when you were done with the lesson, they were free to go. A win-win.

There were two male students in particular in that class, the names of whom I can't remember, but the nationalities I do—one was Greek and one was Vietnamese. The former was born in the U.S. to immigrant parents, but did live for several years in Greece. The other was an immigrant with the rest of his family. One of the text books we used had various readings in them, designed more to provoke thought in students and to be used for writing exercises. One day we got on the topic of "What makes a person happy?"

But Larry the Greek and Sam the Vietnamese (those names are as good as any) became the impetus for this writing assignment I used in class one day. I think the reading had to deal with getting a good education to get a good job, the "be all and end all" of Western Civilization. Larry couldn't quite grasp that concept, for in Greek culture, your goal in life was to get married and have a home and family of your own. Maybe a car. But these were the very basics of a happy life—not money or education.

Interesting.

I asked Sam to share with us what life was like in Vietnam. It was even simpler than the Greeks—they would work each day, long enough to earn the cost of their day's food. When that happened (whether at 10 a.m. or 3 p.m. or 6 p.m.), they were done working for the day. They went back home, ate, and had fun—playing cards, singing, whatever. But it was a communal effort—there were always others there to be with.

So that became my spur-of-the-moment essay topic—each student had to write an essay to explain what it is they wanted in life that would make them happy, or make their life complete, or fulfill them. Whatever. But three pages, due Friday.

Too bad I didn't accept my own challenge. Here it is, nearly twenty years later, and I still have no clue what would make me happy. The world is my oyster and I come up empty. I just know I'm not happy. What is the cause of it? What is the reason for it? I don't know. Can I fix it? Probably—if I knew what needed to be fixed.

Advice For The Lovelorn Pakistani

This must be why people are so dependent on friends—they help you sound things out and also offer hindsight or an objective (or subjective) opinion on what your problem is. I don't have many friends, most certainly no confidants, but there are *plenty* of people who tell me what my problem is. And it isn't *my* problem, but their problem I am being blamed for.

My life really wasn't bad. Lonely, but I was used to that. Once my sister left home, almost immediately after graduating high school, she married and they moved to California. They were doing all right for themselves. But there was nothing here in Indiana for them, except family. They liked the idea that this was their homestead, their roots were Hoosier through and through. But they had a life to live and who could blame them? I was too young to really go anywhere—this is all I knew. Life was good. My mother and I had a roof over our heads, food on the table, a color TV, and Bingo on Saturdays. What more could a person ask for?

A lot.

I don't know what I want, but I do know what I don't want.

Marriage and children were never an option—I didn't want them. Growing up without a father figure, or even a male figurehead—I just didn't get why they were in charge. They were fascinating creatures, but I never really had a desire to own one. And after a few years of living alone with my mother, I realized I was stuck. Not in Indiana, but with her. She was raised to be a housewife and mother, before the term "stay-at-home mother" entered the lexicon. Women were *expected* to stay at home, raise the kids, take care of the house. She had no skills and now she was just old enough to be excluded from the workforce. She could never support herself. It dawned on me, at the age of thirteen, it was up to me to take care of her.

That doesn't mean she didn't keep trying to marry me off to any of the single men who played Bingo on Saturdays—marriage is what was expected for women. In her mind we were a package deal—she'd pick him out, I'd marry him and give her grandchildren, and she'd live, with us, happily ever after.

With two failed marriages under her belt, I somehow didn't trust her on this. The fact these men were spending Saturday nights playing Bingo with a bunch of old women, most often their own mothers, wasn't a selling point. Besides—she had grandchildren in California. She doesn't call them or visit them, why on earth would she need more grandchildren?

"Well, they're not from you."

Is that supposed to make a difference?

After I graduated from high school, it eventually dawned on me that the topic of most Bingo conversations was about expected grandchildren. Teenage daughters were pregnant, oh woe is us—what shall we do?

"Get her an abortion," my mother would say.

The women would laugh—*isn't she funny?* Always kidding around. They would look at my stoic expression and ask me directly, "Is she this funny at home?"

"No," I would reply dully. "And she's not kidding." And they would respond with more peals of laughter.

Times were changing. Marriage was more of an option, not a pre-requisite for parenthood. But my mother was old-fashioned. A woman married, had children, and stayed home to raise them.

Silly me—I was working! Supporting myself! Who would watch the kids? Certainly not my mother. She needed the sitter herself. Actually, more of a servant—someone to drop everything and do her bidding when she demanded it.

And that's when it dawned on me—the insistence on my getting married and having children—she needed something to brag about at Bingo.

After one particularly annoying discussion at home, she once again asked me when I was going to get married and have children.

"You're just jealous," I replied. "You're the only one at Bingo who doesn't have an illegitimate grandchild."

And just like that—the discussion was over. The only thing worse than my not having children was not having a *husband* to have them with.

Chapter 2

"Jane, would you do me a favor?"

I was startled by the voice—it was Frank. He rarely spoke, except to the other male professors and only then to talk about baseball. I was shocked he knew my name.

"Well, I had to ask John what your name was. I'm not good with names."

Really? We've shared this office for half a decade and you barely acknowledge my presence. I would not be surprised that he didn't know my name, but to ask John—and he knows his name? Is he a male chauvinist pig or what? And—the fact he's only speaking to me because he wants a favor? So many things to say—do I err on the side of valor and keep my mouth shut? Naw.

Besides, my brain and mouth have never been connected.

"You're a real charmer, Frank."

Frank blinked three times and his weight shifted from the balls of his feet to his heels. If this didn't scare him off, he must be desperate for help. My help. I noticed he was holding some papers in both hands, which he began to curl. I gave a sly smile—I'm fluent in sarcasm and sarcastic looks. I swiveled toward him in my office chair. "What's the favor?"

He tried to smile and act casually. *No wonder I don't have any friends. I shoot them down the minute I get them within my sights. What's wrong with me?*

"Well, uh," he kind of laughed. His right eye continued to twitch. "I was wondering if you could take a look at this for me. Since you teach comp, you're a genius with words."

"I wouldn't say I'm a genius, but I'd be happy to take a look. What is it?"

Seeing his opportunity, he pulled up his chair and sat down. He was very tall and thin, and the chair could easily seat two of him. *Some people have all the luck—my kingdom for a working metabolism.* He put the papers on the desk and smoothed them out with both hands, his long fingers trying to uncurl the damage he did.

"My wife is working on cover letters for a job search. Now that our little guys are in school, we decided it's time for her to begin working outside the home . . ."

My head was swimming. *Wife? Little guys? As in, you have children?*

And, oink—we decided it was time for her to begin to work? Oink.

"—and I always hear you and the other girls—"

Oink. "Michelle and Erin?"

"Right." He wasn't sure how to react. "But I always hear you ladies—"

Much better.

"—talking about your students writing résumés and such, and I thought, if you wouldn't mind—"

"Sure, I'd be happy to help."

I felt like a kid on Christmas. This was insane. I was getting a peek behind the curtain. I began, almost too casually, asking questions. *Too bad I can't write this information down so I can tell Michelle and Erin. That would be too obvious. I hope I can remember it all.*

Yes, he's married, just celebrated their twelfth anniversary. He has three children, a girl and two boys. Ages eleven, nine, and six. All three love baseball. He spends his evenings outside with them playing catch. Crap—what was it he said about the dog? Oh, and his wife's letter.

After this, Frank did speak a little more to me, mostly when there were fewer people in the office, but it was a start. We could almost have casual conversations, which were mostly about the weather, but it was a dialogue. And his wife did get the job. Over the years, she worked her way up to a pretty important position and was given more responsibility.

All thanks to me.

Chapter 3

I met Anita first, the semester during which I turned forty. She was beautiful—thin, with a beautiful olive complexion, almost like milk chocolate. She was inquisitive, eager to please. But, she spoke with a very thick German accent. I just couldn't understand that. I had never been to Europe, but I did know two Germans, one being my aunt. A true Aryan, blonde hair and blue eyes. She was born in 1938 and did have memories of Nazis, albeit from a child's perspective. I do remember her talking about "high German" and "low German." I'm not sure if that meant the dialect or the accent or the color of their skin. I thought Germans were all white. Maybe Anita was a "low" German, from near the southern border. After all, in the southern United States, many people do have darker skin, whether they're blacks or Hispanics. In my mind's map of Europe, the border was the mark between Germany and Yugoslavia or something like that. I didn't know any Slavs at the time, so maybe I was right. It took a few days before I discovered the truth.

She wasn't German.

This didn't solve my problem—it only exacerbated it. It took another few days to get an answer.

Her husband is German.

Argh! So how is it she speaks with a German accent?

She lived in Germany with her husband.

Okay, that makes some sense. She lived there for ten years; after ten years, you would start to pick up the accent. I can understand that. But, she explained, German wasn't her main language, it's her third.

Uh-huh.

English is her fourth. The first two are Spanish and Portuguese. She's from South America and "everybody speaks Spanish or Portuguese."

English is her fourth?? How can I teach her anything? She's smarter than I am!

Anita was born in Brazil. Anita grew up in Brazil. Anita met her husband, Fritz, in Brazil. The company he worked for in Germany sent him to Brazil to work on a project and that's where he met Anita. When his job called him back to Germany, Fritz married Anita and she moved with him to Germany.

I must keep repeating and emphasizing Brazil because, the untraveled Midwesterner that I am, I confuse it with Argentina, and I break into song: "Don't cry for me, Argentina . . ." Basically, Anita is from somewhere in South America. All those places look alike from here.

But they're not.

And I must keep repeating Anita's name because I keep calling her Evita. And then immediately break into song with even more dramatic emphasis, raising my right arm, palm facing upward, "Don't cry for me, Argentina . . ."

That's probably why I keep thinking Anita is from Argentina. I love that song. Any old excuse to break out into show tunes, I guess.

As a college professor, I live and die by my seating charts in class because, point-blank, I'm terrible with faces. Names I can remember, but visually matching that name with the face it belongs to just doesn't happen, at least for the first six weeks, and sometimes longer. In general, when you see people less than an hour every other day or even just once a week, it's hard to keep them straight. And for some reason, it's worse with men. They all look alike. And God help me if they actually take off their John Deere (or New York Yankees, or Chicago Bears, or whichever team they're rooting for) hat. I have no idea who these people are. I feel like I've just been blindfolded and I'm swinging the bat for all I'm worth, but that piñata is nowhere to be found.

And it's worse when you have multiple classes and the students all have the same name. There was the one year I had three Michaels in the same class, and of course they sat next to each other. Then there was the year of the two Tylers, in different classes, but they sat in the same seat. And there was enough of a physical resemblance where I had no idea which one was which. And then the class with a Karissa and Corissa. So the seating charts are a must.

Students find it hard to believe that a teacher may not easily recognize them, and I am always reminded of what a teacher of mine told our class one day when he couldn't remember a name: "There's one of me, and I have a hundred and fifty of you to remember. Give me a break!"

So for the first several weeks, if I'm not looking at the seating chart, I will often inadvertently call people the wrong name. It really isn't intentional. I want to keep the energy flowing and I think I can remember simple names.

Famous last words.

So, in my brain, it's all the same. Brazil and Argentina, Anita and Evita.

Po-tay-toe, po-tah-toe.

The lady from South America did not agree.

Maybe that's why she calls me by my last name all the time.

In my defense, I did try referring to students by their last names such as Mr. So-and-so and Miss What's-your-face until the semester all of the students, to quote my colleague Erin who had a class earlier in the day than I did, reported that "Everyone this semester is from Poland." When I checked my roster, it was true. Many last names had a lot of consonants with the pairing of the "sz" and ending in "ski." That was also the year I met Greta, but I'm getting ahead of myself.

But Anita was (and still is) a perfectionist. But this is in a good way. She puts in the effort to earn this status; she doesn't blame others when perfection doesn't magically appear. Anita soaked up everything, especially when it came to her writing. The more corrections I made to her work, the happier she was. As her writing got better, and she had fewer mistakes, she was sure she was failing the course because of the lack of fixes.

"But you got a ninety-seven out of one hundred. This is the highest score in the class."

"Ack, I don't know about that," she modestly replied in her thick German accent. "But, Smith, are you sure this word is correct?"

And then the task of trying to explain auxiliary verbs . . . And this was how I began to notice when an ESL student was in my class. They would have perfect grammar and punctuation, but incorrect verb form.

And yes, I know the term "ESL"—English as a Second Language—is now politically incorrect. And I know it's been adjusted at least twice since then. I think one less-offensive variation was "ELL"—English Language Learner. But you get the idea.

If only the American-born students had such a grasp of our language.

Two stories in our anthology dealt with "cultural illiteracy"— how little we (twenty-first-century Americans) know as a culture about history, geography, anything really. Late-night television shows often have segments featuring the program's host stopping random people and asking them simple questions, like how many moons does the earth have. Answers would vary wildly. (And the correct answer is ONE.)

But one particular story in our anthology had twenty questions right off the U.S. citizenship test. It was always a fun lesson (well, at least for me) on the day when I would give my class a pop quiz on those little tidbits of information.

Here they are:
1. What are the colors of the American flag?
2. How many states are there in the union?
3. Can the Constitution be changed?

4. For how long do we elect the president?
5. How many branches are there in the American government?
6. How many senators are there in Congress?
7. What is the Bill of Rights?
8. Who said, "Give me liberty or give me death?"
9. Which countries were our enemies during World War II?
10. Who elects the President of the United States?
11. Why did the pilgrims come to America?
12. Who wrote The Star-Spangled Banner?
13. Who was the main writer of the Declaration of Independence?
14. What special group advises the president?
15. What is the minimum voting age in the United States?
16. When was the Declaration of Independence adopted?
17. What kind of government does the United States have?
18. In what year was the Constitution written?
19. Where is the White House located?
20. What is the introduction to the Constitution called?

Simple, *n'est-ce pas?* *

I would jokingly begin, after they had written their answers down, by saying, "Okay, let's see how many of you we're shipping back tonight." There would be some very nervous laughter. You could see them mentally preparing their packing list. As well they should have—some of them should have been sent back, they knew so little about their country. But—if this is a good enough test for new citizens, shouldn't the natives know this information as well? **

Advice For The Lovelorn Pakistani

As the semester progressed, Anita invited me to lunch.

This was a first for me. No student had ever asked that of me and when I was a student, I never would have asked a teacher to associate in a social manner. I guess I'm very old-school (no pun intended). Classroom decorum doesn't translate to human status. And you hear so many stories about inappropriate relationships . . . it's very definitely something to think twice about.

But I liked Anita. I was honored to think she would want to be my friend. I thought about it and told her I would prefer to wait until the end of the semester and after the grades were submitted. As hard as she was working for her grade, I didn't want even a whiff of favoritism to be associated with either me or her. Of course, she earned an A and we made our plans. (And when I say she *earned* the A, I mean just that. As I tell students—I don't give grades, you earn them.)

She invited me to her home and there were four of us: Anita, myself, Anita's daughter Davina, and Phyllis, who was also a colleague of mine at CHU. She taught French at the university, but she also volunteered as an ESL instructor at the local library, which is where Phyllis met Anita. I knew Phyllis on sight and the most we ever spoke was more in passing (either she was arriving for class as I was leaving, or vice versa). Davina was eight years old at the time and just a pleasure to be around. She was intelligent and articulate and very respectful of adults. *(Note to American parents—follow this advice! Trust me, your kids are not as cute as you think they are.)*

Anita had studied art while a young student in Brazil and took a few courses when she lived in Germany. Examples of her work were plentiful in her home. What a talented woman! Oil paintings of all types of subjects were on display in the beautiful home. They were not overpowering in color or placement, but very subtle. They just blended in perfectly with the décor of each room. Many of the scenes included mountains and rivers, some reflecting the landscape of South America, some reflecting the landscape near her home in Germany.

Our "quick" lunch lasted four hours. It was one of those pleasant June days in Indiana where the temperature was warm, the breeze was gentle, the sun was bright, and the humidity was low. The conversation flowed and the laughter was plentiful. What a wonderful day and a wonderful end of the semester. Anita survived her first semester as a U.S. college student. She had already registered for the fall semester and was nervous.

"I just don't know how I will manage all of the reading for these courses," she sighed as she showed us her schedule. Psychology, Sociology, Introduction to Business Practices, World History, and English Composition 201.

Phyllis and I looked at each other. "Are you insane? You're taking five classes?" *Odd, that sounded like my voice saying those words. Did I speak that out loud?*

"I must be," Anita agreed. "I almost lost my mind this semester." She showed us her grade report: English Composition 101, Calculus, U.S. History, and Public Speaking. Straight A's.

Phyllis and I again looked at each other. Anita has a beautiful home, immaculately clean. She cooks three meals a day *from scratch* for a family—she has a young daughter, a preteen son, and a husband—she's carrying a full load of classes, and she's aced every last one of them. *I wonder if I can bottle her?*

But looking back, I must smile. We had this exact same conversation every single semester she was a student at CHU and even as she worked on her MBA. Each semester, Anita called me the first week after she had attended her classes and received the syllabus for each of the courses, with all of the work spelled out. The conversation had a familiar pattern to it: the classes were the hardest she had ever taken, she had no idea how she would survive the courses and what was she going to do?

And every semester, she had the highest grade in each class, she made sure daughter Davina and son Donald were more active with extra-curricular activities (and Anita attended every last one of them), and her home was still immaculate. I don't know how she did it. I was just in awe of her.

And I still am.

Okay—stumped by the citizenship test questions? Here are the answers:

1. Red, white, and blue
2. 50
3. Yes
4. Four years
5. 3
6. 100
7. The first 10 amendments
8. Patrick Henry

9. Germany, Italy, Japan
10. The Electoral College
11. For religious freedom
12. Francis Scott Key
13. Thomas Jefferson
14. The cabinet
15. 18
16. July 4, 1776
17. Republican *(I personally accepted bicameral, but this is the answer the Feds want. Just in case you really need to take the test.)*
18. 1787
19. Washington, D.C. (1600 Pennsylvania Avenue, NW)
20. The Preamble

*N'est-ce pas is French, roughly translated to "isn't it."

* In 2019, as this book was being prepared for publication, the State of Indiana passed a law that Hoosier "High Schools will have to administer the U.S. Naturalization test, as part of a mandatory government course, that's given to immigrants hoping to become U.S. Citizens. An initial plan had proposed that students had to pass the test to earn their diploma, but that plan was scrapped."

I was just ahead of my time!

Chapter 4

Maybe it's just me (I'm sure it's not), but there seems to be that one person you always run into. There was a family of six that I would always run into at the Laundromat. I went at 7 a.m. Sunday mornings, the time they opened. It nearly killed me at times, but it was the only time I could really set aside to get laundry done. The nice thing about Laundromats is that all the clothes are washed at the same time and you can dry it all at the same time. There are plenty of machines to go around.

But there was a family each time I was there which sticks in my mind. It was a mother and father and four young boys, probably between the ages of four and ten.

I can never forget how well behaved the children were. They sat on the bench, they talked quietly. They never ran around, they never whined. They behaved. The way it should be.

I don't think the parents and I ever spoke, but we "knew" each other enough to know which machines and dryers we used, and we respected the space we each used.

Sophia was one of those people, like this family, who I would run into quite a bit.

Sophia was a woman I would see in various classes I took as I worked on my master's degree. She was taking classes for hers as well. We knew each other as classmates, but I really got to know her better when we were paired up for a class project as part of a group.

Sophia was an anomaly in my life. She was everything I had hoped existed somewhere in this God-forsaken world. She was musical. I loved music. She loved to read. I love to read. She loved to write. I wanted to write. She loved to try new things. I was open to anything—if it wasn't for the constant monotony, I would have no life. Sophia was organized. She was professional. Everyone wanted to be just like her! I wanted to be like her. This is what I want to be when I grow up—Sophia!

This was so exciting—I had not lost my mind! There were actual human beings in this world who did all of these wonderful things like read books and listen to music. I was no longer a freak of nature. She could back me up! And on her it worked. There was hope for me yet.

Sophia was the eldest of six children, the only one to have attended college. She had a deal with her parents—if her siblings wanted to go to college, she would help pay their way. The parents had paid for her education and this was how she was going to repay them.

"That doesn't seem very fair," I said. "They're not your children."

"Oh, I think it's very fair," she said. "After all, I was the eldest. The least I could do is help them with the younger ones. Fortunately, none of them wanted to attend college. But if one day they do, I will honor my promise to my parents."

See? She's different!! Who would do something like that?

Her family was very close. They celebrated everything together. A birthday was a family dinner. When one of the children was going to prom, everyone went to the school to watch the grand march. If one of them was in a sporting event or a school concert, most of them would attend. Definitely the grandparents, several of the aunts and several of the cousins would be in attendance. They supported each other and stuck together. That's what family is about, isn't it?

At least that's what I've seen on television.

But the thing that struck me as odd about Sophia's family is they didn't worship her as much as other people did. Everyone loved Sophia and truly admired her. People wanted to be her, not just me. But with her immediate family, she wasn't the star. And this became painfully obvious to me when she won a scholarship to take a sabbatical and study in Europe for a year.

Europe! As in across-the-ocean-to-the-continent Europe!

I would offer up a major body part and possibly kill someone for the chance to go to Europe. But to spend an entire year there? I couldn't breathe. I was breaking out in a cold sweat. And it wasn't even happening to me!

After we had both earned our master's degree, Sophia kept taking classes on various subjects. She earned enough credits to become endorsed to teach foreign language. The school where she worked needed someone to teach Spanish, so she taught a course of that. As she added more to her studies, and the student enrollment grew, she began teaching more courses in Spanish. Then she added French to her studies and to her teaching load. As I said, she's an amazing woman.

Who has the stamina to take a three-hour course at night after a full day of work, not to mention caring for a family on top of that? I couldn't handle a seventy-five-minute class in the evening, and I had no real responsibility other than putting up with my mother. Due to her age and just for convenience more than anything, I was still living at home. I did the yard work, she did most of the cooking. Neither one of us did much house cleaning. I come from a long line of slobs, I admit it. It was just easier to not have anyone come to the house for a visit.

But Sophia worked very hard as a teacher, continuing her education—everything she touched turned to gold. Everyone she worked with and associated with was always impressed by her. Her parents? Her siblings? They had absolutely no interest in what she did. It didn't bother Sophia in the least. How could it not? It annoyed me and I barely knew her family.

She shrugged. "It's just the way they are."

"Okay," I replied, more than a little confused. "Which is what? How?"

"It's not just them, it's everyone in this area."

I wasn't sure I fully understood where she was going with this. The area where we were living was known for its heavy industry, in particular, steel mills. Years ago, you could quit school at sixteen, get a job in the mills, put your thirty years in and retire. The workers had good, high-paying jobs and a cushy retirement. During the 1980s the steel industry went into a steep decline with cheap imports of steel from Japan. Keep in mind the Japanese steel mills were built after the devastation of World War II. The steel mills in the Calumet Region were built around the turn of the twentieth century. They were old, inefficient, and took several men to run. The more modern, efficient mills in Japan didn't need that many people to work. So men lost their jobs and the future of the steel industry, as well as the region, became very bleak. The workplace now had a very different look. Computerization of the steel-making process meant a worker would need a college degree. No more high school dropouts were needed, and the high-paying jobs they could rely on were going to college grads.

And if you're going to the effort to go to college, why would you want to work in a filthy, dangerous steel mill when you could earn more money working in a nice, cushy office?

So, while this scenario of high-paying, low-skill jobs was no longer the case and hadn't been for nearly thirty years, the mentality still existed. While I dreamed about traveling to, or even living in, New York City and Europe, the rest of the local yokels couldn't wait for the next three-day weekend to drive home to Kentucky or Alabama or Mississippi where the rest of their kinfolk lived. They were called "down homers"—they'd drive fourteen hours down home, stay for thirty-six (most of which was spent sleeping), then drive the fourteen hours back home.

I couldn't relate. We were from Chicago and had no "kin" left up there, so I could never fully appreciate this quaint little ritual.

But, in a way, that was exactly what Sophia meant. She was very patient with me as she tried to explain her family and their behavior. "People who live around here do not value a higher education or opportunities to better themselves," she explained. "But I do. I had students who would earn full, four-year scholarships to prestigious universities, and they never finish. They usually are back home within six weeks."

"None of them graduate?" I exclaimed. "As a teacher, aren't you supposed to push higher education?"

"Oh, yes, and that's why it's maddening. But it's the leaving-the-herd mentality."

She went on to explain, but it turns out I did understand the concept, I had just never given it a name. Many families in this area are very close-knit, and most are first-generation (if that) high school graduates. Once a person turns eighteen or graduates, then it's time to get a job, or get married, but either way you had to support yourself. That's what their parents did, that's what their grandparents did before them, and by God, this new generation, the ones who were Sophia's students, were going to do it as well. Most of the children lived in the same town as their parents. Few members of the family rarely traveled farther south than the county seat, and even fewer to the next county. They were physically as well as mentally close.

"In fact," Sophia explained, "I have cousins who live in the next county, but my siblings have never visited their home or have even seen them in twenty years because of where they live."

"What, do they think they'll need passports?" I asked. She laughed.

"They must. But any place that involves an interstate for travel, they won't go."

"So where do they go on vacation?"

She shook her head. "They don't. They stay home. The husbands will go to Tennessee to hunt or fish, but my sisters stay home. They'll visit our folks, play with their grandkids. They have no interest in anything outside of this area."

Sophia found herself outside the herd when she left for college. Even though she lived within two miles of her entire family since her graduation, she left the herd to go to school downstate. And even though that's what her parents wanted, deep down they really didn't. Going to college meant she was better than them. Not that she ever lorded over them or made them feel bad, but they knew in their hearts she was better than they. And to go to Europe? On purpose? No, they couldn't take that. For everyone else it was a dream come true, for them, it was a waste of time and money.

Like there was so much here in the state of Denial. I mean, Indiana.

And I can't entirely blame them or Sophia. My mother was the same way. Why go anywhere—you're risking a plane crash. Or a car accident. You can be killed here at home so don't waste your money. And what would happen to me if you died?

Well, if I'm dead then it's not my problem, now is it?

And do we really have to wonder why I'm not married? I don't leave the house. We never have guests. We never go anywhere and consequently I have no social skills. So how the hell would I ever meet a man unless he happened to walk up and knock on the door?

The never-ending refrain and cycle of rhetorical questioning. Stop the world—I really want to get off.

Chapter 5

As I entered my forties, my mother died. I'm almost ashamed to admit it, but I didn't cry. I cried more when I had the cat put down years later than I did for her. I liked the cat.

Don't get me wrong—I'm not happy about her death. You must remember this basically was my only parent. My sister and her family were living in California and they came back for the funeral. Then they went back to their life and I went back to mine.

Except I really didn't. I didn't have a life to start with. I just didn't know it at the time. My schedule for the past decade was arranged around therapies and doctor visits for my mother, and this new-found freedom threw me for a loop. I can go away for a weekend. I can go out after class with a co-worker.

Holy crap, I am free!

But, like a dog that is used to being attached to a certain length of chain, my little world only went so far. Sophia was now an empty-nester so we spent more time together. This was a wonderful adventure for me. I could go out to dinner at the drop of a hat—I didn't need to be home! I could go to a concert

Advice For The Lovelorn Pakistani

or a lecture in Chicago with Sophia! I could do things! What an incredible time in my life.

But the more time I spent with Sophia, I learned that "leaving the herd" is a true mentality. It's almost as if you are being disloyal to the family. And you feel obligated to keep their respect, so you tamp down any ambition or emotion or thought that would lead you away from home.

Me, on the other hand, it was all I thought about. But I didn't have the drive, and maybe the ambition, to leave. Lacking the money was also a reason, but I digress. I was stuck and I knew it from the age of fifteen. I was stuck in Indiana. I was stuck with a mother who was quite content to play the victim and wallow in her little existence. It was my job to keep her comfortable in that situation. And it was my job—nay, my duty—to get married and have children. Not for me, but for her. This way *she* could benefit. But I wouldn't wish her on my worst enemy. And to get married, I would probably have to leave the house to find a man. They weren't breaking down my door. And I worked with mostly women, so that wasn't even a possibility. But I knew there was life out there, somewhere. Save yourself, E.T., because I sure as hell can't save myself.

Now, I need to explain Chicago. Indiana's motto is "Crossroads of America," and that is true. In one city, four major interstates are located within its boundaries. At one point, Interstates 80, 90, and 94 are all the same stretch of road. (*Can you say congested?*) So to go to Chicago is a major ordeal. You don't just "go" to Chicago. Oh, sure, thousands of Hoosier residents commute to Chicago every single day for work, but regular people don't even think about attempting it. I can never get there in less than three hours and I live three miles from the Illinois border. It's the amount of traffic, the crazy Illinois drivers, the crazy Indiana drivers, and the thousands of trucks transporting goods to the east coast from the west and then to the west from the east coast. Needless to say, there are very few two-lane roads in this area, unless you're driving through a subdivision. But every subdivision has at least one semi-driver who brings his work home with him.

I even knew people, other than Sophia's relatives, who refused to travel on the interstates. As one friend explained her reluctance to drive on the highway, "There are cars there." And no, she wasn't blonde.

Sophia was used to driving into Chicago. She had attended dozens of lectures and concerts and even was a frequenter of the Chicago Symphony Orchestra as well as the occasional opera. So she was always the chauffeur on our adventures. I would drive to her home, park my car and hop into hers. She could get up there and parked and into the building in under an hour. I don't know how she did it. Well, the getting into the building part I do know—she walked very fast.

My soul just grew by these experiences. I was hearing live music. I was meeting authors. I went to my first opera with her. We saw silent movies with a live orchestra playing the score. I can't imagine the hours of practice for that orchestra to be able to not only perform the music so perfectly but to also keep in synch with the movie.

Advice For The Lovelorn Pakistani

Sophia was very easy to talk to. It also helped that she did most of the talking. I loved listening to her stories. And it was on one of our drives to Chicago that we decided we were going to Europe. She longed to go back, and I just longed to go. As luck would have it, the planets aligned and an opportunity presented itself. Sophia was going to France one summer to take a course just for fun. (*Who does that? Isn't this the most exciting thing a person could do? I want to be Sophia when I grow up!*) Once her coursework was done, why not fly over with her daughter, Lauren? Then the three of us could tackle the continent.

I nearly swallowed my tongue. Everything I had ever hoped for was coming true. And even though I was a novice traveler, Lauren was not. Sophia made sure to show her the finer things in life (like culture, art, music, traveling) and the high school where Sophia taught and Lauren attended often had European trips for foreign language students. Lauren had graduated from college a few years before and did spend a semester studying in Europe as well. I was in very good hands.

Sophia left on June 1, shortly after her school year ended. Lauren and I would fly to Paris on July 23. I didn't think July would ever arrive, let alone late July. What would I do between the end of my semester and the trip? Teach summer school.

Now, I had never taught summer school. I had never even attended summer school. I completed all of my studies, from elementary school through high school and even college, during the school term. (In my defense, I think this was because there weren't many options during my high school years to take courses during the summer unless a student had flunked a course.) And I didn't think that I could teach summer school—

didn't they have their stable of professors doing that? Every story I have ever heard about teaching summer school said it was easy money for the faculty, and those with the most seniority were lined up to rake it in. But this summer there were no takers. This would be money and a diversion for me, so I happily accepted.

It was basically a sixteen-week semester condensed into eight weeks. The class would meet two evenings a week for seventy-five minutes a session at Central Heights University and it would be worth three credit hours. In fact, it was the same course I had been teaching, English Composition. What could be easier?

The sixteen-week course would be easier. Did I mention I was teaching Advanced Composition?

CHU's writing program showed no mercy to its students. Under the theory that the more you write the better you become, students wrote multiple drafts of each paper. And by writing multiple drafts of each paper it would foment a practice within a student during their academic career to work on each and every assignment in multiple drafts so the finished project was as perfect as it could possibly be. There were five assigned essays (not counting the smaller, daily journal writings which were only a page a piece, for every credit hour per week). A 750-word-draft was due every Friday, the last class day of the week. That allowed the professors a weekend to grade the papers to return on Monday. A revised draft would be turned in the following Friday, that corrected draft returned Monday, and a final, revised draft would be submitted that third Friday. This was the money paper—the one that fully counted. So five papers with three drafts equals fifteen weeks. The sixteenth week would be the final exam.

That's a lot of grading. Even with the maximum class size limited to twenty-five students, and over four classes, that's one hundred papers (provided all of the students turned one in).

Hmmm. This might be another reason why I'm single—who had time for a social life grading one hundred papers every weekend?

Now, if my math is correct (and I am not good in math), at minimum, a semester provided up to one hundred students each turning in a paper each week for sixteen weeks. But this was summer school, with twenty-five students doing five papers in eight weeks and multiple drafts . . .

How can they do multiple drafts when we have eight weeks? Maybe only do one draft?

Cutting the number of essays was not an option. But fewer drafts were all right. And the journal writings.

So forty-five journal writings of one page each times twenty-five students over eight weeks with five essays with more than one draft, carry the one . . . Damn, I really wish I knew algebra. But it's probably a good thing I don't, otherwise I would have convinced myself it was impossible, like I do with truly inconsequential things that can be easily accomplished. It is true what they say: Ignorance is Bliss.

Somewhere lost in the translation and discussion about taking on this class was the part about how the hell to pull it off. Other than cutting one draft of each essay out, I literally taught a full sixteen weeks in eight weeks. And, God love them, the students worked their rumps off and kept up with it. It nearly killed all of us, but we did it.

And yes, I did have a foreign-born student in this class. She was a young woman from Hong Kong who was called Kenny. I have no idea what her proper name was (and let's be honest, I probably couldn't pronounce it if I did know). She was educated in China and had emigrated to the United States. She never said a word in class.

Until that one class discussion, the one about higher education, reared its ugly head.

The students were sharing stories about their respective high schools. There was a fifty-fifty mix of suburban schools and rural schools. One thing all had in common—there was at least one teacher, usually a coach, who either favored the athletes and gave them no homework, or showed movies everyday and gave students no homework, or the teacher who offered a worksheet that would be more fitting for an elementary student (it was that easy) and this allowed the students to sleep in class. Yes—that was another common trait—sleeping in class and getting away with it. Oh, and getting an A.

It made me cringe. My high school most certainly was not like that.

Kenny raised her hand and asked permission to speak. *Of course! This was a class discussion and you most certainly are part of this class.* I was relieved that she was going to say *something*!

And say something she did. This was when Kenny exploded. And I mean *exploded*.

"Do you know what students must do in China?" she said loudly, through gritted teeth. Her teeth may not have actually been gritted—she was biting her words and her enunciation was flawless, her accent fairly mild.

Advice For The Lovelorn Pakistani

"Students in China must take six classes, and each class you are given two books like this," she held up her index finger and thumb about two inches apart, "—and you must memorize each book. We are only allowed to go to school for eleven years. At the end of the eleventh year, you must take a test on each subject and you must memorize the book. And if you pass those tests, you may attend for one more year of school. If you don't pass, you must then go to work."

"So they can just go to college later?" one of her American classmates asked.

"Oh, no, they cannot. If they do not pass this test they are not given the letter that will permit them to go to college. They must go to work. Their school days are finished."

There was stunned silence. It could have been because this was the first time Kenny was actually speaking, but I would like to think it was a cold slap in the face of what American students take for granted.

"And then," Kenny continued, "if you get that twelfth year of schooling, you are given twelve new books that are this thick—" her fingers now three inches apart, "—and you must memorize these new books. And at the end of the twelfth year, you must take six new tests. If you pass these tests, then you can go to university. If you don't pass those tests, you must wait two years before you can try again."

"And then they can go to college?"

"No! Not without the certificate."

"Then what do they do those two years?"

Kenny was a little calmer, but still wound up. "They may work, or they can leave the country and go to school. Many come to America to study. You must wait two years before the test. You can take the test as many times as you need to, but you must wait two years."

Among the many things circling within my head at this time was a recent news report about how superior Asian students were to the rest of the world. The statistics showed how Asians were far superior to American students. Americans were actually offended by this news and preparing to boycott imported items. How dare the world say we're stupid! We're 'Muricans, dammit!

But after listening to twenty American high school graduates, who were proud of the lack of challenge they had to face, and then listening to an Asian student explain her situation, I had the proof of that study's validity right here in this classroom.

And by the end of this summer session, I was exhausted. A nine-hour, overnight airplane ride would be a godsend. I needed the sleep.

I had my suitcase in the car as I drove to CHU to submit the grades (*yes, boys and girls, this was required to be done in writing, not submitted electronically. Ah, the dark ages of 2004 . . .*). I don't remember sleeping much that week, but I walked them to the registrar as quickly as I could (I don't run), hustled back to the car, then off to pick up Lauren and catch the bus for the airport.

Sophia was going to meet us at Charles de Gaulle Airport in Paris when we landed the next day. She would take the train to Paris with her luggage, which was very common for people to do. Owning a car in Europe is more of a luxury in some places but they also have a phenomenal public transportation system. She had rented a car, which she would pick up at the airport. After our excursion, we were all booked on the same flight back to the States, so we could easily drop off the rental car. She really knew what she was doing. She planned nearly everything to the final detail. To her, this planning was second nature because she had done such traveling with students and had to have everything squared away before she could even send permission slips home with her students to have their parents sign.

Our flight was uneventful and even so, I wasn't able to sleep much. Maybe it was the excitement, maybe it was the newness of the adventure, maybe it was because I was so tired that the adrenaline that was keeping me going was still pumping through my body. We left in a dark evening sky from Chicago at 9 p.m. and arrived the next day in a very bright and sunny Paris about 11 a.m. We made our way to baggage claim just as the items from our flight were beginning their journey on the conveyor belt.

The second suitcase to appear on the conveyor belt from the flight was mine. I squeezed through my fellow travelers to snatch it off the moving belt and tried to maneuver out of the way of the others who were waiting to get their suitcases. I told Lauren I could stand with our carry-on bags apart from the crowd since I had my suitcase. That way she could go closer to the belt for her suitcase without juggling the smaller bag. I found my spot about six feet away, leaving plenty of room for the crowd at the luggage carousel.

I relished these first few moments on European soil. After sitting for so many hours, it felt good to stand. I shifted my weight between both feet and looked around. Things at de Gaulle were similar to what I knew from domestic airports, but hearing the different languages being spoken, watching the people, I fully realized that deep down, we are all alike. I noticed the windows and was taken aback by the flag pole in front of the airport. How odd to see the tricolors rather than the Stars and Stripes. I realized that I really was a rookie at life—I've never seen a flag pole without the U.S. flag on it before. It took a few moments for me to fully comprehend this.

The crowd around the luggage carousel and conveyor belt was thinning, but there were about fifteen people still waiting, including Lauren. Apparently, an entire cart load of luggage was still sitting in London. It would be loaded on the next plane to Paris, the airline personnel promised everyone.

Wait—London? As in England? How did it get there? We never landed there.

That's when I learned that if a flight has too much cargo, cargo becomes interchangeable. If it doesn't make one flight, it would go on another. From there, they would coordinate to get it to its proper destination, ideally before the owner of the cargo arrived. But sometimes it doesn't work out that way.

Like now.

"This happens every time I come to Paris!" Lauren moaned.

"How often is that?" I asked. *Every time you come to Paris? What an odd choice of words. How often do you come to Paris?* I couldn't relate.

"This is the third time. The first time was when we came on vacation," she said, about the first trip to France she and Sophia made when Lauren was twelve. "The second time was when we took a class trip in high school. They lost it then. I was the only one in the group without luggage. And now, this time."

I did feel bad, a little bit. I had mine and it's hard to feel bad when you're not inconvenienced. I was very grateful my bag made the trip with me on the same flight. But it is also hard to generate a lot of sympathy for someone so young who has trouble "every time" they come to Paris. That would be like me saying "every time" I go to the grocery store I would invariably be stuck with the worst cashier ever hired by anyone. It was a bad analogy, I admit, but I'm blaming it on the jet lag. And maybe a little jealously.

The big fear was that Lauren had put her cell phone in that suitcase, the cell phone equipped to be used in Europe. How would we contact Sophia? Within moments, Lauren said, "Never mind, there she is." Lauren walked away, leaving me standing there looking like Europe's worst nightmare: A jet-lagged American tourist.

Never mind what? There who is? Where did she go?

Sophia, the always prompt and vigilant Sophia, was there! When she arrived, she began walking toward baggage claim. She was calling my name and even waving her arm, beckoning me over to where she was standing. I literally did not see her. I was in Paris—I don't know anyone here.

She and Lauren went to an airline representative and learned the next flight over the Channel was airborne now and would be landing within the hour. They could not verify if the suitcase was on that plane. Sophia was optimistic and it was decided we should eat lunch here at the airport and wait for the bag.

They had a Burger King in Charles de Gaulle airport in Paris! My little Midwestern brain was about ready to explode. This was just too surreal for me to comprehend.

We found a table in the dining area near a window and Lauren filled Sophia in about what was going on at home with the dogs, the parents, the siblings, the mail, life in general. I was silent as it was taking all of my concentration to chew my hamburger. What was wrong with me? I'm not a connoisseur savoring taste. I've eaten a hamburger before. It's not like a French burger is different from an American burger, especially at Burger King. How long does jet lag last?

Sophia described the rental car to us. It was smaller than she had hoped, but sufficient. Almost as an afterthought, she asked me, "You drive a stick, right?"

Do. I. Drive. A. Stick?
Like a stick shift.
In. A. Car.

I think I grunted when I finally comprehended. "No."

"Never?" Sophia asked, a little surprised.

"No-o," I responded. I really must have bad jet lag. I thought my response to the question "Do I drive a stick?" was pretty clear and to the point. Maybe I misunderstood. "Why?"

"Because cars in France come with a manual transmission because of the mountainous terrain." Sophia looked at her daughter. "You can drive a stick, right?"

"I haven't since I was sixteen. But I can pick it up again."

Sophia and I looked at each other, eyebrows raised. "No," Sophia said, "you are not going to try to 'pick it up' driving through the Alps."

Advice For The Lovelorn Pakistani

With only one driver now, instead of three, the original plans would have to change. While we waited for Lauren's suitcase, Sophia opened a map she had in her shoulder bag. Italy was out, Switzerland was out. We would head into Germany for a short trip and then spend the remainder of the time in France. Our eventual Bavarian destination: Munich.

Such detail and such planning—all I could say was "Aye, aye, Captain!" I think I even saluted. I mean no disrespect—this was so exciting, and it sounded so simple. Sophia appreciated the moniker and, as she often jokingly called me "Professor," Lauren began to giggle. "Well, we have our Skipper and our Professor, so do I get to be Ginger or Mary Ann?"

"More like Gilligan," Sophia teased her daughter.

"How about Little Buddy?" I offered. I was starting to make sense—the jet lag must be waning. Or the caffeine from my drink was kicking in. I was becoming coherent. As much as I enjoyed watching *Gilligan's Island* in reruns, it's not an image people want when you're on a trip. After all, those seven people were just going on a three-hour tour.

A three-hour tour.

That little earwig ended up becoming the theme of our trip. *Welcome to Europe, Jane Smith.*

A few days later, after our arrival in Munich, Lauren and I raided the hotel's rack of brochures for tours and events happening in the area. Both of us had expressed an interest in seeing Dachau, the infamous concentration camp which was near

Munich. In fact, one company offered three daily tours, leaving at various hours. "We could do this in a half-day," I said, not thinking. "It's only a three-hour tour."

Lauren and I exchanged a glance. We both knew this was not funny: The hundreds of thousands of innocent people who were forced to enter those gates absolutely had no humor in it. Then why were we thinking of that other three-hour tour made popular on television?

Our Skipper piped up. "I've heard about those tours. You have no problem getting a bus to Dachau, but it's difficult getting one back."

"Isn't that what they told the Jews in 1944?" *Did I say that out loud?* Lauren tried not to laugh. I bit my tongue.

"What?" Sophia asked. At this, our Little Buddy laughed out loud. Sophia did not see the humor and she admitted she was only half-listening. She had been told by other tourists who actually did travel to Dachau on those tours that they had a difficult time getting back on the return bus. But, always the Skipper, we could add a trip to Dachau to our itinerary and, as we had the rental car, we could visit there on our way back to France.

"Oh, well, that will work too," I said. I looked at Lauren, and continued in a quieter voice, "At the very least they can trace the rental car if we don't return."

She laughed again.

We decided to return the excess pamphlets back to the hotel lobby while Sophia showered. As we placed them in their respective slots we discovered one we missed the first time: a half-day tour of "Hitler's Munich." It could be combined with the Dachau tour for a lower price. "What is that tour about?" Lauren asked.

I glanced at the brochure, paraphrasing. "Munich is near and dear to Hitler's heart because he lived here, blah blah blah."

"Near and dear to his heart?" Little Buddy was near hysterical with laughter. After studying in Munich for three months while she was in college, the city was also near and dear to her heart. But, she hoped, that was where the similarity ended.

But the first order of business was booking a tour to Salzburg, Austria. *Austria! I'm going to Austria! As in the birthplace of Mozart Austria! As in* The Sound of Music *Austria!*

As in Not Indiana!

Salzburg was actually fairly close to Munich. The tour was billed as an all-day affair, lasting about eight hours. It would leave first thing in the morning.

I'm going to Austria for eight hours! Alert the media!

We boarded the bus about 8 a.m. and were told we would be returning to Munich about 7 p.m. "That means this is an eleven-hour tour," I said. Our tour guide announced we would be taking a boat trip on Lake St. Wolfgang, which was the difference in time. A difference of three hours.

"Okay," I said, "call me paranoid, but we're going on a three-hour tour, involving a boat?"

"You're paranoid, Professor," the Skipper said. Little Buddy was in the seat in front of us, already fast asleep.

Our walk through Salzburg was wonderful for me; others might not be that impressed. We didn't go into any of the buildings due to the lengthy lines to get into any of the Mozart-related locations such as the museum and birthplace. Clark, our tour guide and bus driver, pointed out the buildings related to *The Sound of Music*. We saw the mansion up a mountainside, the church was outside of town and was more of a drive-by viewing as we headed to Lake St. Wolfgang. "Look to your right—that little building was the church," Clark said. But I didn't care—it was closer than I've ever been to these things. Baby steps, Jane, baby steps.

Words cannot adequately describe the majestic beauty of the Alps, the blueness of the sky, or the serenity of the lake. I had never experienced anything quite like it. We had some time to walk through the quaint town of St. Wolfgang before returning to the rest of our tour group at the pier. This wasn't the south Pacific, but it was a paradise.

"Our boat ride will take about thirty minutes and the bus will meet us in St. Gilgan," our tour guide said.

The Skipper looked at me. "Did he say Gilgan or Gilligan?"

Before I could answer, a small motorized boat approached the dock. I couldn't believe my eyes. It was a small, white boat with an enclosed cabin in front. I began searching the boat, looking for the name of it. It surely couldn't be . . .

"Well, we can now say our ship has come in," Little Buddy giggled.

"Is it me, or does that not look like the S.S. *Minnow*?" I asked.

The tiny ship was not the *Minnow*, in either name or behavior. There were plenty of seats on the deck where the passengers could sit and soak in the grandeur of the scenery. If there was one place to be shipwrecked, this was it—the blueness of the sky, the coolness of the breeze, the colors of the flowers in the window boxes of the chalets. It was a perfect view.

All the tourists returned to the bus for the trip back to Munich. It was a hot day, and the bus was even more so, being locked up while we were sightseeing. Sophia, Lauren, and I were seated on the upper deck of the bus, along the back, where there was a five-person bench. We opted for that rather than two seats together, separated by the aisle, since there were the three of us. Clark, who was the only American besides us on the trip, apologized to everyone about the temperature. He assured all of the passengers that the air conditioning would soon kick in and cool the double-decker bus. It would take a while before the cool air rose to the top deck and he offered people seats on the main deck. A few descended, but we stayed put. We didn't have air conditioners at home, and Europe isn't known for its artificial cooling systems, so it wasn't an unbearable situation.

Before we crossed the Austrian-German border, the bus pulled off the road. The motor was still running, but I noticed Clark had exited and was pacing frantically along the side of the bus, toward the back of the vehicle where we were sitting, out of sight of the other passengers. He was speaking on a cell phone.

"This can't be good," The Professor in me whispered to The Skipper.

Suddenly, the bus motor stopped running. The silence was almost deafening, and the heat was stifling. Not wanting to cause a panic, because we weren't sure how much English the other passengers understood, Sophia and I looked at each other and mouthed the words, "This can't be good."

I again looked out the window.

Clark was pacing even more frantically, speaking on the cell phone.

I tried to mentally do the math, which as I've said isn't my strong suit. We were about two hours away from Munich. It was rush hour. By the time a new bus came to pick us up and return us to Munich, it would likely be about four to five more hours. Not exactly the three hours that we should be stranded, but enough with the coincidences. Five hours is more than three hours and therefore there is no connection with that certain television show. And besides, this was a bus, not a boat.

The bus soon started and shortly we were on our way, sweltering. Nothing was explained to us until we returned to Munich hours later and Clark told The Skipper that the bus had overheated. Even with the air conditioning off, it was still in the danger zone. That's why he had pulled over and tried to call the office. It was suggested he turn off the motor for ten minutes and try again. He was able to nudge it along, slowly, through the Alps to Munich. Ironically, the trip ended after ten and a half hours, not the eleven hours proposed at the start. So, no three-hour increment.

"Are you ladies planning any other tours during your stay in Munich?" Clark asked.

"Yes," The Skipper said, "tomorrow we are doing the castle tour."

"So am I," Clark said. Sophia and I smiled. Clark was handsome, somewhere around middle age. It was just a bonus to we two single women. "But there are two tours going out tomorrow—mine and one solely in German. Make sure you get on the right bus."

"Oh, we will," I said, semi-flirtatiously. "See you then!"

Where did that come from? I'm flirting with total strangers in Europe?

As we were heading back to the hotel, congratulating ourselves on our luck at having Clark as our guide for two tours, Little Buddy Lauren couldn't take it anymore.

"You two are acting like a couple of forty- and fifty-something-year-olds."

Sophia and I stopped and looked at each other. *Was that an insult?* Granted, the truth hurts—we were in our forties and fifties—but it kind of begged the question: *What should we be acting like?*

"Jealous?" The Skipper asked her daughter.

"You say that like it's a bad thing," I added. Lauren sighed and walked ahead of us. Sophia sped up, trying to keep her in view. We had lost her twice already on this trip, both times on our first day while touring a church in Reims, France and later in Strasbourg. Lauren wasn't really lost; we had just lost sight of her for several minutes.

"Give me that cow bell you bought in Salzberg," Sophia told me. "We need to tie that around her neck."

The next day we toured two of the castles of "Mad" King Ludwig. We would begin at Lindenhof castle, go to Oberammergau for a short visit and then to Neuschwanstein castle where we would spend three hours.

"Does it seem like we have a recurring theme going here?" I again asked.

A second theme began to emerge during the visit to Lindenhof, but I couldn't put my finger on it. King Ludwig was mad, and also very weird. The king had a tree house on the grounds of Lindenhof. He was a huge patron of the arts, especially composer Richard Wagner, even having a piano specially built at Lindenhof for Wagner, at taxpayer expense, of course, which Wagner never played.

Lindenhof was also referred to as a mini-Versailles. Ludwig was a Francophile, and the decorations inside and outside the castle attested to this. One room had a wall of mirrors, there were portraits of the French royal couple throughout the palace, and even a fleur-de-lis made out of flowers behind the castle. *It was almost like he never grew up*, I thought. Granted, it was 2004—things were very different during the 1800s.

As we traveled to Neuschwanstein, we learned more about the Bavarian king. He was born August 25, 1848.

August 25? Why does that date sound familiar?

He died under mysterious circumstances at age forty. He was engaged but never married. For some reason, the portraits of the king in his military uniform looked familiar to me, but I wasn't sure why.

Clark explained what the tourists should do while at Neuschwanstein. Their tour of the castle was at 3:15, so they had time for lunch. Then, pointing up at the top of an Alp, the passengers on the bus got their first good look at the castle.

"It may look familiar to you," Clark said. "Walt Disney used this castle as a model for Cinderella's castle at Disneyland. And even though the castle here sits more than eight thousand feet up, you can still hear the bells of the cows in the valley at that distance."

"But how will we know which one is our Little Buddy's?" Sophia said to me, not missing a beat. Our Little Buddy did not see the humor.

We left the bus at the bottom of the mountain. Clark said there were two options up the mountain: one is the shuttle bus, which is always packed, and if you planned on taking it, you should not eat lunch at the restaurant due to the length of time you would wait for an empty bus. The bus would take you to the castle, but it would also drop you off near *Marianbrueck*—Marian's bridge—which traversed a ravine which gave an excellent view of the castle. Clark highly recommended doing that. The bus didn't go to the bridge, but it dropped you off about a five- to ten-minute walk away.

The second option was to walk up the mountain. That would take about an hour and a quarter, if you were in shape.

"Sounds like we're doing lunch and taking our chances on the shuttle," Sophia said.

Luck was with us—we not only ate lunch, but also got a ride on the shuttle bus up the mountain to Marianbrueck. As advertised, the bus left us a short distance from the bridge.

After a few minutes of walking up an incline, I declared, between heaving puffs, "If anyone asks, we hiked up an Alp. Granted, it's only for five minutes, but it's up and it's an Alp. This counts."

When we arrived at Marianbrueck we were greeted by a character that can best be described as Heidi's Grandfather. The old man, in dark green lederhosen and matching green felt alpine hat, with grey hair and long grey beard, did add a lot of flavor to the scenery. He also took photos of the tourists on the bridge (for a small fee) with Neuschwanstein castle, across the valley, in the background. How could we say no?

And why am I thinking of the troll who runs the toll bridge? Or was that The Three Billy Goats Gruff? *Man, I need to reread those fairy tales. They do come in handy sometimes.*

Inside the castle were photographs of the construction site, during the late 1800s, where men were building the castle on the top of an 8,000-foot mountain, without machines. They were also wearing bowler hats—talk about formal! It was an amazing concept to behold. There were several portraits of Mad King Ludwig throughout the castle as well. Lauren passed me and said, "He looks like Michael Jackson in those military outfits."

That was it! I looked at the portraits of King Ludwig II. That's what had been driving me crazy. The second theme to the trip was the Michael Jackson connection with Mad King Ludwig. The Treehouse at Lindenhof. The military uniforms. The August birthday. Cinderella's castle vs. Neverland Ranch. *Could Jackson be the reincarnation of the Bavarian king?*

After we returned to our hotel, I told Sophia and Lauren about my theory. Sophia arched her eyebrows and began to plan for the next day's adventure. Lauren offered more support. "Both were eccentric," she began. "And wore military uniforms.

"Both had trouble with women," I said. "Ludwig never married, Michael never should have."

"He's the King of Pop and married the King of Rock's daughter, which would make Lisa Marie a princess, right?"

"Right. And the King of Pop versus The King of Bayren. Oh, and the brothers," I said. "Ludwig's brother is Otto, Michael has Tito."

"Both of them spent money on crazy things," Sophia added. She smacked her head—*Why was she getting involved in this conversation with these lunatics?*

"Both weren't well liked in their home towns," I said. Living close to Gary, Indiana, the hometown of the Jackson family, I knew emotions ran more cold than hot toward the family. Lauren added, "Ludwig was obsessed with Paris, Michael named his daughter Paris."

"Enough!" Sophia said.

The final full day in Munich would be spent at a chateau called Nymphenbourg by everyone except me. For the life of me, I couldn't remember the name. I knew it had something to do with nymphomaniacs and came up with Hypo-nympholand. The site held many attractions. Aside from the museums, chateau and gardens, there was the Magdalene chapel, which Sophia wanted to visit. She had visited Nymphenbourg before, but was not able to enter the chapel.

Two new themes emerged this day. We had become accustomed to everything happening (or so it seemed) in three-hour increments. The Michael Jackson-Mad King Ludwig connections had slowed down considerably. One new theme was that the homes used by the former German royal family were all referred to as mini-Versailles, and Nymphenbourg was no exception.

As we entered the grounds of Nymphenbourg, we noticed a strange phenomenon. Hundreds of white seagulls were on the lawn, but only on one side. We walked down the path bisecting the lawn toward the castle.

"Isn't that strange?" Sophia said about the birds.

"I wonder why they're all on that side," Lauren asked. We stopped to look. Nothing was on the left side of the lawn. The right side of the lawn was almost totally white, being covered by the birds.

"Must be union regs," I said, looking at my watch. "It's 12:05. They probably switch sides on the hour."

As we toured the castle, I took advantage of an open second-floor window to look out over the grounds. About half of the seagulls had migrated to the other side of the lawn. I looked at my watch: 12:30.

After touring the castle, we walked outside to the grounds behind and started down a path with the sign for the Magdalene chapel pointing left.

"I know a shortcut," Sophia said. And off we went, to the right.

After all of the wise decisions and accurate knowledge she had displayed thus far, the final theme of our trip began to emerge: Our Skipper's debatable sense of direction.

Advice For The Lovelorn Pakistani

The path was nice, at least it was shaded. The day wasn't humid, but it was hot.

The shade provided much needed cooling. Lauren wondered aloud why people would be allowed to just roam the grounds, since this was a castle. Weren't they afraid of vandals hiding until dark? Or, being Americans, are we just less trusting of people?

"There are probably cameras planted in the trees," Sophia mused.

"Probably disguised," her daughter continued. "Hey, look at that snail!"

They stopped. *What snail?*

Lauren pointed to a tree. There it was, at eye level. "Sure it's not a camera?" I asked, always the skeptic.

We peered closer. The organism was moving, even the tiny antennae. "Nope, it's real," Lauren said.

As we continued down the path, Lauren found more snails on the trees. One tree had five snails on its trunk. "That's probably the camera tree," I observed, pointing at the slightly curving line of snails. "Five snails? Look at their angle. A little suspicious."

To our right, there was a real camera, under the bottom branches of a tree, about ten feet above the ground.

"That must be the fake one then, huh?" Sophia asked.

"But of course. That is too obvious. They wouldn't have a real camera be a camera," I said, always one for conspiracy. We trudged on, Sophia in the lead, Lauren slightly behind, me a few steps farther back. For a non-hiker, I was keeping up, for the most part. And they also were learning to walk slower.

"SNAKE!" I yelled.

They stopped. Another second later and Sophia would have stepped on it. "Where?" she asked.

It had already slithered into the brush.

"Awww," Lauren said. "It was just a little garter snake." *Had she even seen the thing?*

"*Little?* That thing was *huge!*" I said, probably near hysteria. To say I was not a fan of snakes would be an understatement.

"It was a baby," she teased.

"Its body was the width of my fist. That's not a baby."

Lauren smiled to herself and began to tease me in earnest. "So, what exactly are you a professor of? If you're this freaked out by little bitty garter snakes."

I tried to take a deep breath. In truth, I was half afraid she would double back and try to find the thing. "Writing! You know, the three R's? And no, the R's are *not* for reptiles!"

None of us dared to look at the other for fear of laughing. Yes, I knew I sounded ridiculous. But it was a really big snake.

After about ten more minutes, we came to a brick wall.

Literally.

Lauren and I looked at each other.

A beat.

Sophia pointed to the wall. "The chapel must be that way. We'll have to go around."

"There was that sign," Lauren said.

"Where?"

"Before the snake," I mumbled.

"Where we started," Lauren added. "The sign pointed the other way."

"Ah, well, then, we'll try that," our Skipper said.

So back we went, past the snails, the half mile back to the sign pointing to the chapel. Once there, we began the trek anew. This new path was three-quarters of a mile there and back. *So, let me do the math—if we went a half mile and back, that's one mile, plus another three-quarters, and back. That's like two and a half miles? In a single outing? Egads.*

The Magdalene chapel was a small, brick building built in the 1720s. We crossed the foyer into the chapel, which was entirely covered in coral and sea shells. According to legend, Mary Magdalene emerged from the sea on the southern shore of France, after the crucifixion of Jesus. The entire interior of the namesake chapel was covered with items from the sea. Shells of various shapes formed designs on the coral—intersecting curves, straight lines, etc. Small stones formed the outline of bricks on the wall, with smaller stones filling in as the grout between the bricks. The colors on the walls were pastel—tans, yellows, blues, greens. Even up in the cupola were seashells, outlining the panes of glass, with the blues and greens covering the exposed brick. It was a beautiful sight. It was definitely worth the walk. Not the snake-sighting part of it, but definitely the two-and-a-half-mile part of the walk.

We returned to the mansion to explore the attached museums. It was now 2 p.m. and the seagulls were back on the right side of the lawn.

One museum contained King Ludwig's various forms of transportation: The carriages, sleighs, and a merry-go-round.

A merry-go-round?

Sophia and Lauren had already turned the corner and entered another wing when I stopped dead in my tracks.

I'm seeing it, but I don't believe it.

To the left side of the doorway into the next hallway, there was a lighted glass display case, with three shelves of noses in various states of disrepair.

Oh no. It can't be. Not noses.

An older man sat on a folding chair by the merry-go-round, across the room from the glass case. I went over to him. "Do you speak English?"

"A little," he replied.

I pointed at the case. "What's with the noses?"

The man explained it was part of a game the king and his guests used to play. They would ride on the merry-go-round and attempt to shoot a nose off a Roman statue. He pointed to a stone bust on a pedestal near the ride. There were small brass arrows, about six inches long, which riders would use to try to score. He pointed to an example on display. It was something akin to the modern-day pastime of grabbing the brass ring while riding on a carousel.

That's why the noses were in such a state of disrepair—some people had better aim than others.

I was relieved. No connection whatsoever to Michael Jackson and his many mishaps with his surgically-altered schnozz.

But, naturally, I can't keep this information to myself. I went after Lauren and Sophia. I found Lauren first.

"I don't want to go back there, I just want to get out of here," she said, whining with exhaustion.

"Not until you see this. It's worth it."

I related the story of the noses, the merry-go-round, and the old man who spoke just enough English to tell the story. The man watched us, not understanding what was being said, but knowing he was part of it.

"Oh, my God," Lauren said between laughs. "Did my mom see this?"

We went to find Sophia, who was also looking for us. "Where were you two?"

"You have to come see this," we said in unison.

"See what?" She was skeptical. She had visited this museum before and was fairly familiar with it. What could there possibly be that was so important?

"The case of noses," I said.

"Case of noses? I thought you two were done with the Michael Jackson references."

"Not anymore," her daughter replied.

We escorted Sophia back to the glass case. The old man stood in the corner looking nervous. *How many more of these Americans were there?*

We soon finished our tour of the museums and began heading to the exit. It was three o'clock.

"Hmm," I said. "A three-hour tour."

"And look at the seagulls," Lauren said. They were still all on the right side.

"They didn't move," I said. "They should be on the left side. It's the odd hour."

"I wonder why they are doing that to begin with," Sophia wondered aloud.

Moments later, we learned the secret. A little boy walked through the grassy area and the birds scattered in fright, over to the other side.

"I guess that explains that," Lauren said.

"I guess the birds are as goofy as Ludwig," I said.

We headed back to our hotel to pack for the journey back to France. We would be flying home in three days. There were no more three-hour events, no more Michael Jackson connections, and the next mansion we visited was the real Versailles.

We never did make it to Dachau. But that's okay—I went to Europe!!!

As luck would have it the next summer there came another opportunity to go to Europe. Lauren's college was offering a cruise of the coastal cities on the Baltic Sea. Most ports of call were limited to just hours, but we would spend two full days in Russia.

Russia!

We would fly into Berlin.

Germany! And Berlin! By now the Berlin Wall had been torn down. *Holy cow—we would get to be in East Germany. Remember that?* The country was unified now, but it's bragging rights if nothing else.

Advice For The Lovelorn Pakistani

After traveling up to the port on the German coast and boarding the boat—

"It's a ship," Sophia corrected me.

Po-tay-toe, Po-tah-toe. It's a big boat, all right?

From Germany, we would stop for about six hours in Gdansk, Poland.

Poland! And in the birthplace of Solidarity! Lech Walesa, here we come!

From there we'd travel for a day at sea before landing in St. Petersburg, Russia.

Squee! Where the Czar lived! And I was just reading a book about Nicholas and Alexandra, the last Czar and Czarina. Talk about a coincidence.

The next port of call would be Finland for an afternoon. "That's all?" I said.

"Bragging rights," Sophia said.

Then we'd go to Stockholm, Sweden, for about six hours. And after spending the final night on the ship in port in Stockholm, we'd depart from there for home.

Bragging rights, indeed. Now all I need is someone to brag to.

Chapter 6

Needless to say, our second trip was wonderful. It was so exciting to see places I've only seen on television or read about in books. My soul was awakened and my horizons became broader. I finally felt qualified to be a college professor, even though I had been one for years. I suddenly felt I had more wisdom. I no longer had to live vicariously through my students who were foreign born.

And that's another thing—why was I always getting foreign-born students in my classes? Anita told me her schedule was changed because the bursar wanted her to be in my class. I have never met the bursar, so I have no idea why. Maybe it was that first successful encounter with Sam and Larry—word got out that I was patient with students like this? I have no idea. But the only student I was still in occasional contact with was Anita. I would help her by proofreading her essays and I would occasionally see her on campus, depending on our schedules. Ironically, Anita graduated just before Sophia and I took our first trip, so I would pick Anita's brain about Germany and living in Europe. She was all too happy to give me advice and explain things.

It's not like we were going to be spending so much time in each location, but it helped her to share her stories with me.

"The people here, the Americans, they're really ignorant about Europe, eh?" she asked.

Anita was blunt, but she was observant. I then got to explain about the tunnel vision that afflicts many of my countrymen. But she was happy I was finally achieving one of my dreams to travel and gave me enough information for six trips. It would have been wonderful for her to join us, but she and her family were celebrating her graduation with a quick trip to Germany to visit her husband's family about a month before our trip, and then she was starting graduate school with the summer session. But she was my cheerleader and I was hers.

That fall was when I met Greta. This was the semester where my colleague Erin observed, "every student was from Poland." I was teaching another writing course, this one in the evening at a local high school, not on campus. Both were firsts for me. I was used to commuting to campus and teaching for fifty minutes, or for seventy-five minutes if the classes met two days a week. But three hours in one sitting was going to take some getting used to. It only met once a week, so the entire week's lessons would need to be taught the same night. No time for them to reflect on work, or do it and bring it in two days later.

Ironically, Greta was from an area near Gdansk, Poland. Sophia and I were just there on our cruise! I thought it was more than an odd coincidence that I no sooner return from there and find one of them as my student.

Greta was in her mid-thirties, married with four children. Her youngest had just started kindergarten and Greta wanted to become a teacher. Her husband agreed, so she was taking one course to begin with. She knew she would be in her forties when she finished, but this was a journey and not a sprint. And, as English was her second language, which she had only been speaking for about fifteen years, she wanted to make sure she could comprehend the readings and adequately do the writings before taking on more courses.

It turns out this class of mine was perfect for her. Of the eighteen students, nine of them were mothers—women with children *(as opposed to what, you may ask)*, as opposed to the other students, male and female, who were "typical" college students—late teens, early twenties. And this came in quite handy about midway through the semester when I decided to do my "deserted island" lesson.

Where I got the idea for this, I don't really remember. It had to be from a comedy television show. Maybe it was an improvisational comedy show. Anyway, the premise is this: Your group must begin civilization anew, or you're forming your own country—your choice—and you're allowed to have ten items. What would you choose?

When I had done this exercise previously, I had divided the class into males and females. The females were more practical, choosing things like food, shelter, clothing, medical items, education, etc. For the guys, it was usually beer, beer, beer, beer, beer, beer, beer, television, women, beer. I then made them prioritize their list and we would discuss their choices, allowing time for proper heckling (mostly by me, but in a nice way).

The points of this lesson were many—organization, prioritization, combining, argument. Great qualities for any writer.

Well, this time I decided to try an experiment: Mothers vs. Others.

The moms chose the usual things my female students had in the past. As mothers, and as females, they selected very practical and very nurturing items. For the Others, maybe it was because half the group was female, rather than it being an all-male group as I've had in the past, but they broke the mold and actually chose items in a similar vein. One of the items the Mothers had selected was a police force—something for protection and keeping the laws. A member of the Others, a young man named Paul, scoffed. With such a small group of people, why would you need a police force? Wouldn't everybody know the rules and then know who broke them? For Pete's sake, there's only nine of you.

After analyzing the Mother's list, we then began critiquing the Other's list. Paul was the spokesman for the group. His group mates were young and didn't care; they just wanted class to be over with so they could go home and watch television. But Paul was just beginning to feel his young oats and was really enjoying this exercise and his newfound authority.

We got through items 1 through 5 fairly easily. Items were more common sense and very similar to the Mothers' list.

Then we got to Number 6: Military.

"Why a military?" I asked Paul and his group.

"Because you need someone to enforce the rules," Paul replied, matter-of-factly.

I looked to the Mothers, who looked at me. *Didn't we just have this conversation? And more specifically—didn't we just have this conversation with Paul?*

"But why a military," I persisted, "and not a police force?"

Paul explained his thinking, but I wasn't fully convinced why you would have need for a military and not a police force. Wasn't a military a little extreme? I kept trying to rephrase the question. The Mothers took a stab at it as well, trying to ask him the right question to unlock the mystery.

Paul was a very sweet young man. He was nineteen and beginning to find his voice. He was developing opinions and was learning how to share them. The problem was, he was nineteen.

As the questioning continued, we could tell by the look on his face that he really hadn't thought this idea of a military force through. It made perfect sense to him, but under the glaring light of reality and the questions from others, he realized he missed something. And the more he thought about it and tried to explain it, the more frustrated he became. I thought he looked as if he was ready to concede. He wasn't.

How does one save face?

"Communism!" He banged his hand on the desk. "That's what we need! A communist government."

Greta, who grew up under Communism, without missing a beat very politely said, "Oh, no, you do not, and here is why."

I don't remember sitting down, but at some point I sat behind the teacher's desk and watched the tennis match ensue. Greta explained her position, Paul explained his, and back and forth they went. Very politely, very determined, never raising their voices. All of our heads bounced back and forth between the pair. It was probably a good thing they were seated at opposite ends of the classroom. After a while, the other students looked at me. I was dumbfounded. All I could do was shrug my shoulders. I had no idea what was going on. I had never seen anything like it. They don't teach you this shit in college.

This went on for ten minutes. Then fifteen. Then twenty. Then twenty-five. Finding the briefest of lulls in their discussion, I told them to go take their evening break and threw them all out of class. As this was a three-hour class, we would take a break at about the half-way point, which it now was. They ran out of the room as if their lives depended on it. I tried to think of where I was going to go from here. This night definitely was one for the books. I'd never experienced anything like this.

Within just moments, no more than fifteen seconds, Paul returned to the classroom. He had a bag of candy in his hand, retrieving one at a time and eating it. (If it were me, I would have poured the whole bag into my hand and then put the entire contents into my mouth. Or just bypassed the hand and dumped the entire bag into my mouth. I am both fascinated and annoyed by people who eat each item individually. I guess I'm just normally a glutton.)

But why was Paul here? Of all the people, why was he back in here so quickly? My heart sank. I really needed a break. What happened in the hallway? Was I going to have to get out of the chair and . . . be a responsible adult? I didn't hear any commotion, so I was hoping . . . hoping what I don't know. Hoping I didn't have to get out of the chair, I guess.

"What happened?" I asked, dreading the answer.

Crunch, crunch. "I didn't have enough money for the vending machine." *Crunch crunch.* One candy after another he pulled out of the bag, popping each one individually into his mouth.

I looked at him—*if he didn't have enough money, how did he buy the candy?* The *crunch crunch* continued. *Crunch crunch.*

"So how did you buy the candy?" I asked. *Please, God, don't let him have taken his frustration out on the vending machine . . .*

"She gave me a nickel so I could buy my Skittles." *Crunch crunch.*

"Who?"

"Her." *Crunch crunch.*

"Greta?"

Crunch crunch. "Yeah." *Crunch crunch.*

By now the other students, still shell shocked, were slowly filing into the classroom.

Do you mean to tell me that the fate of Western Civilization was saved by a nickel and a bag of Skittles? Where's Kruschev and his shoe when you need him? Does the UN know about this? Think of the billions we could save in military costs each year!

When everyone had returned, I picked up from where we left off, with Number 6. Within ninety seconds, they agreed with a final order of items and we were done with the lesson.

Skittles, huh? I guess Moms know what kids need and when they need it.

On our class syllabus, Central Heights University insisted that all professors give their students contact information. I included an e-mail and my cell phone number. Even though I still had a land line, there are times when you need some privacy. I could always turn off the cell phone.

Advice For The Lovelorn Pakistani

Greta would occasionally e-mail me. She would ask questions about the assignments, but often she would see a picture or a cartoon and share that with me. She loved my sense of humor and I was flattered she would take the time to scan an item and e-mail it. This was during the dark ages of the time before Facebook and iPhones, and people still regularly read newspapers. It was the best of times.

As our correspondence developed, she felt comfortable asking questions from an educator standpoint. She wanted to be a teacher, so she was using me as inspiration. I'm not sure if I should be flattered or terrified. There were a few times when I was running late or had a meeting on campus, and I asked her to get the class settled in and give them an assignment to work on until I arrived. She was so excited to have this responsibility. Her classmates were supportive because she seemed to know what she was doing. She already had the teacher persona.

Greta was thoroughly enjoying life as a college student. She was so determined to succeed. She worked so very hard and everyone in the class just loved her. The next semester, I was given a class again at the same high school, one night a week for three hours. This time it was a Wednesday night class. Greta was taking public speaking, which was down the hallway from my class, also on Wednesday nights. She would occasionally pop in before class or during a break to say hi and have a quick chat.

It was on Ash Wednesday when Greta popped into my classroom before class began that evening. None of my students had arrived yet and I was unloading the items I would need for the lesson from my satchel. It took me a few moments to realize there was something on her forehead, and a few more to recognize what it was—a cross made of ashes.

Now, I didn't grow up in a church or with a lot of religion. Ash Wednesday was just Wednesday to me. Sure, I saw the stories on the newscasts about Chicagoans going to Holy Name Cathedral on Ash Wednesday to have ashes placed on their forehead, but I was baptized as a Baptist. I didn't know many Catholics, so I never actually knew anyone who did this quaint little ritual, let alone ever see anybody with this on their face. Most of the people in my community were Protestants and we never ran into people who did this. The Catholics I went to school with went to church after school, so they wouldn't have to explain the mark (or probably wouldn't be made fun of because, after all, we're teenagers and it's something different). It's just one of those things you hear about but don't actually see.

It wasn't until I was in my late twenties that I actually saw someone with the cross on the forehead. She was a former co-worker. After a few of our co-workers changed jobs, we started a sort of supper club where we would gather once a month for dinner somewhere and catch up on everyone's life. We always met on a Wednesday because that was payday. So the one Ash Wednesday when we were out to dinner, Mary was sporting her ashes. She was an older lady, already retired in fact, but a very devout Catholic and just the sweetest person you would ever want to meet. That was the first and only time I had ever seen this in person. And Mary kindly explained to all of us Protestants at the table the meaning and ritual behind it.

It eventually dawned on me that Greta, being Polish, was also Catholic. Now it all made sense.

Until Patty walked in.

Patty was a blonde in every sense of the word. Sweet, funny, one of the Mothers from our class the previous semester. She turned forty in November; we had class on her birthday, and she made sure everyone knew it was her fortieth birthday. Patty was also taking a class at the same high school on Wednesday evening, but she wasn't in either one of our classes. She lived in a town that was predominately Baptist, I suddenly realized, as I ended up in the middle of a controversy.

"Oh, my God!" she exclaimed upon seeing Greta. "What's wrong with your face?"

Greta looked at me. *What does she mean?* No one had ever said that to Greta before. Everyone Greta knew already knew what it was—they had the same thing on their face. Maybe it's the language barrier that was confusing Greta.

"It's Ash Wednesday," Greta explained.

Keep in mind, Patty was blonde.

"So?" she asked. Greta looked at me again, starting to get a little desperate.

I was suddenly talking—how, I don't know, because I was trying to comprehend all of this myself. "Some religions will place ashes on the forehead on Ash Wednesday. Today is Ash Wednesday."

"What does that mean?" Patty asked.

"It marks the beginning of Lent," I said.

And then we had to explain Lent to her. Greta again looked at me, more desperate, her big, blue eyes growing wider by the moment. I think my eyes were getting to be as big as Greta's as I tried to explain this phenomenon (and I was only one experience up on Patty) and was running out of things to say because, well, I didn't fully get it either.

"Oh," Patty said, finally comprehending. "When did they start this?"

Greta's eyes were the size of saucers as she shoved her face toward me, pleadingly, to make this stop.

"About two thousand years ago?" I replied. Hell, I didn't know. I couldn't believe I was having this conversation.

"Really?" Patty was amazed.

Mercifully, it was time for them to go to their classrooms. I still giggle every Ash Wednesday, remembering Patty's reaction and Greta's big, blue eyes. Only in America.

Chapter 7

A few years after meeting Greta, I began teaching courses at a second university called Great Northern University, or GNU. To be more redundant, the locals called it GNU U. It's kind of like referring to Automated Teller Machines as ATM Machines. But GNU was urban and so were its students. It was a satellite campus in a city that was eighty-five percent black. Once the white flight in the city began during the late 1960s, it seemed like it took no time at all for the city to collapse into a heap of urban decay. This was before other urban areas began their descent and "urban decay" became a common phrase. What used to be a bustling hub of shopping and commerce became something similar to a war zone in less than ten years. The blacks didn't want the whites there, and the whites didn't want to be there. Clothing stores fled, dime stores fled, pharmacies fled, even grocery stores fled. It's hard to collect property taxes to pay for city services when there is no one on the property. Needless to say, it was a very sad situation.

But this campus was an anomaly. Ironically, its student body was eighty-five percent white, with minorities (which included Hispanics, Asians and blacks) making up the other fifteen percent. The medical courses and programs were top notch and, with the proximity to Chicago, there were more opportunities for work than one would have thought for these young, urban students. But stereotypes do exist and it certainly didn't help that the unofficial motto of the school was 'When our graduates succeed, it's GNUs to us.'

Having taught for years at CHU, a few of the office workers at GNU asked me why on earth I would come to GNU because CHU was a much better university. So much for the pride aspect, I guess. It was ironic in a way because GNU and CHU were the bitterest of rivals. If your parents went to one of them, when it was your turn to enter college you did not dare attend the other one. It was either the alma mater or somewhere else, but never the rival campus.

While I was teaching more advanced students at CHU, here at GNU I had two classes of what were basically remedial courses. They weren't called that. They are listed in a different category, under the "education" department, but these people weren't training to become educators. The official euphemism was "pre-college-level" courses.

You could call them chimpanzees, but once you get past all the euphemisms, they were remedial courses.

The students were admitted to college but not a degree program. They had to pass these classes first. If this were a game of Monopoly, these classes would be "Go."

Many of those taking these classes were non-traditional students, a term used to describe people who were over the age of twenty-five who had been out in the work world for a few years and needed to supplement their education to advance in their jobs, or they were women who had been home raising children and were now ready to focus on their career.

There were plenty of traditional students, those fresh out of high school. They were in college because "that's what you were expected to do," but they were not college material. They had no idea what they wanted to do for a career because they truly had no idea. They just knew they had to go to college. So GNU offered courses in study skills, reading skills, research skills, writing skills. The very basic, but very necessary skills to have in the collegiate world. While they may have gotten out of high school with a D minus, they had to achieve a minimum of a C plus to advance into the degree program at GNU and take their pre-requisite classes.

So, basically, they're too stupid to be in college? No, no, no, I was told, it's not that at all. They're just not ready to navigate the rigors and pursue a degree program. Some just had problems with the preadmission testing, due to nerves or whatever. Whatever, indeed.

Is the university now a farm team for prospective students? Or is it an easy way to make money—the students get government grants to take classes, the university will offer them classes to take their grant money? I have no idea what the truth is. I just know I resented it. I was privileged enough to go to a top university and couldn't get enough grant money to cover it—why were these people allowed to waste grant money on remedial classes that I didn't need with money I couldn't have?

Overall, the students weren't that bad academically. Many had test anxiety and didn't do well on the entrance exams which serve as placement tests for university programs. Some (the younger ones) just didn't take it seriously because they have never taken anything seriously and have always done well. With all of the standardized testing they have completed throughout their twelve years of public education, what's another test? None of them mean anything, why would this one?

I prefer the more non-traditional students because the older they are, the harder they work. They realize they made a mistake by not completing college right out of high school and feel like they are out of the student mind-set. They will do anything you ask them to—just please don't hurt them.

For most of my students, this was the first time they encountered and were in close proximity to people of a color not their own. This goes for white as well as black. This is the biggest and most important lesson they learned, and it didn't come from a book. College really opens your mind, no matter how tightly your parents and family may have closed it. *People are people, no matter the color.* My classes were about a third white, a third black, and a third of non-white/non-black students. It was during my first class that I encountered one of the "others"—head scarf and all.

Fanta was the first real encounter I had had with a student from the Middle East. There was that one guy whose family came from Egypt, I think he said he was born there, but it wasn't obvious. He didn't "look" Egyptian or "act" Egyptian—not that I really know what that entails. Let's just say it didn't affect his outer persona.

As a nation, we were just a few years post-9/11, the 2001 terrorist attacks. Any one from the Middle East still faced scrutiny and for females, they weren't hard to find due to their wardrobe. This area of the nation, the Middle West, can truly be called a melting pot—there are whites, blacks, Asians, Hispanics and every combination thereof. With all the Hispanics, Middle Easterners had the same skin color and, unless you were paying very close attention (none of us were because, well, we're ignorant. There's white, black, and non-white), you really couldn't tell the difference between Hispanics and Middle Easterners. But there were the attitudes that the young people had. Middle Easterners were more modest, polite and studious. Their eyes were larger, a deeper black than Hispanics, and their hair seemed more luxuriant. Subtle differences, but differences to be sure. The females didn't wear dresses, although we Westerners assume they do (that's the Indians and the saris, another topic altogether. And yes, I did have an Indian student, but we never stayed in touch). These Middle Eastern females usually wore vests and loose slacks, almost like pajama bottoms, as opposed to jeans. Those are called shalwar. They are very loose and baggy at the waste and top of the legs and are narrow at the ankle *(note to American clothing manufacturers—we need more of this for plus-size people!)*. Their shirts are called kameez. They are longer shirts, usually without collars, that go below the hips *(again, plus-size clothiers—we need these!)* but those tops do have slits in the side, usually beginning at the waist down to the hem, to facilitate freedom of movement. *(Again—clothiers—it's called "hip space!" Trust me on this!)*

But with Fanta, she was dressed like a "typical" Middle Easterner. She was covered from head to toe in the brightly colored, almost garish, outfits with the matching (or contrasting, depending on her mood) head scarf. Her head, and very specifically, her hair, was covered in a hijab. She had a lovely face. She wore no makeup, nor did she need it. She had the big, brown eyes and rich, olive complexion, a deep shade of brown that wasn't dark brown. Her skin tone was close to that of Anita—a luxurious shade of brown you would associate in a stereotypical way with someone from the Middle East. And she had the unmistakable sing-song accent that you would associate with those from India. She was actually from Pakistan. Close enough.

She was the most attentive and alert student I think I've ever had. She sat in the front row, directly in front of me. She watched every move, listened to every word. She truly was there to learn and to study. She didn't really associate with her classmates. Part of it could have been the maturity level; more than likely it was a cultural issue.

Fanta seemed to favor orange. Her outfits looked very tropical, a stark contrast to the gray, November days that are familiar in the Midwest winter. The clothing material is so thin, I could never understand how she kept warm. Apparently, they wear layers. They're just not visible to others.

The only annoying thing about Fanta was the constant readjusting of the hijab. *Why not just pin the damn thing into your hair to keep it covered?* She had been in class nearly eight weeks before I saw a glimpse of her hair and discovered it was black. And that glimpse was only because we were talking after class and were alone in the classroom. I'm sure if a male student was there this would not have happened.

Her clothing was baggy, as I described early, which I assumed was deliberately to protect modesty. Fanta did explain that was true. The hijab is designed to cover the head, the neck, and even the breasts. The clothing should be loose enough so that the shape of a woman's body is not visible by others. Not all Muslims agree, but generally the face, hands, and feet are allowed to be uncovered. She always wore flat slippers, with the thong to separate the big toe, over a pair of thick and usually very colorful socks. While the hijab matched the shalwar and kameez, the socks clashed violently. But it was an interesting color combination.

Oh, to be young and confident again. Again? I never was!

I remember as a child when they came out with Garanimals for children—easy-to-match pieces of clothing so they never clashed. Just match the animals and your wardrobe was perfect! I had always wished they had Garanimals for adults. Some days I feel as if I need to use a disclaimer when I meet people and they look at my outfit. So in my best, child-like voice, I beam and say, "I dressed myself today!"

By early November, I assigned their final project for the semester, a research paper on a famous person. I gave them the freedom to choose any person they liked. My theory is that if you like the topic, you'll do the work. Especially with a research paper—you're doing a lot of work and spending several weeks with this, so you really want to like your topic. After giving them a few days to think of their subject, I went around the classroom and asked each student who they were writing about. This way, if they had no clue for a topic, their hand was forced. They couldn't waste research time thinking of a topic—they needed to be doing actual research on their topic. While her classmates chose rock stars and movie stars, Fanta felt uncomfortable.

"I want to write about Prophet Muhammad," she admitted sheepishly, in her sing-song voice.

I glanced around the classroom. This was another thing they don't teach you in college—what do you do when something like this happens? I gave a slight shrug. "Why not? He was a person, wasn't he?"

Her eyes lit up, while her classmates' eyes just widened. "Oh, yes, he was!"

"If you don't mind writing it, I don't mind reading it."

I'm always interested in learning new things, I'm just too lazy to do the actual research. When grading research papers, it's pretty easy to tell what has been plagiarized and what are the students' own thoughts. (The writing is so markedly improved, as is the vocabulary.) As much as I like learning new things, I like refreshing my memory on old things. I know a lot about a lot of things. Kind of a Jack-of-all-Trades-Master-of-None mentality. But, hey, it seems to work.

Fanta explained that Muslims believed in Moses and Jesus and the others. They believe that Jesus thought he was the son of God. They just think Muhammad is right.

Sounds reasonable to me.

Part of the assignment was that the last week of class they had to present their paper orally—read it or just summarize it, but I didn't want all that work of research to go to waste. That's been my motto ever since I began teaching. It gives students the opportunity, in a safe environment, to practice public speaking (as well as good listening skills, since I told them if they were disruptive or disrespectful toward the presenter, they would lose points on *their* assignment. Works like a charm.) Also, that last week of class I was pretty well shot, and this was a way to get out of actual teaching.

All of the presentations were awkward—people are terrified of speaking in public to begin with. Some students chose to read their entire paper. Some did very well. When it was Fanta's turn, the awkwardness was at its zenith. The subject alone had people nervous, especially Fanta. She knows what Americans' attitudes are toward Muslims as well as toward Muhammad. And her speaking voice, while loud and clear, had the sing-song accent common in Indians and Pakistanis. I could understand her for the most part, but many of her classmates couldn't process what she was saying. Maybe it was just as well.

But I found it fascinating.

And the only thing I can assume is that this non-judgmental attitude of mine toward Fanta made her comfortable enough to talk to me about her family. Fanta seemed to enjoy our after-class chats. I was fascinated because . . . how often do you get to talk to someone like this? And she worshipped me, being an educator, so it was a win-win for my ego.

Around family, and the males in the family, Pakistani women were a little more relaxed. They didn't wear the hijab and might wear more form-fitting clothing. But she preferred to retain her modesty and honor her parents by living by the Koran. That meant not dressing as a man, or as someone who doesn't believe in God, or by wearing torn or ripped clothing.

Fanta was proud of her heritage and loved her parents deeply. She knew that part of her job as the only daughter was to be in a state of perpetual modesty, and that included her manners and speech as well as her dress. Whereas Muslim women were to keep their heads bowed, this is where Fanta rebelled—she sat in the front row directly in front of me, head up, eyes wide open, ready to learn. I wish I could bottle her for other students.

Fanta was promised in marriage before her family left Pakistan and emigrated to the United States. She really didn't have a problem with that—she said it's what was prescribed in the Koran. Her parents would choose an appropriate mate for her when the time comes, and then she would devote herself to the raising of her children.

"So why are you in college?" I asked.

"My brother wants me to become a doctor, but . . . eh . . . I don't want to," she explained in that melodic, sing-song voice.

"So why do it?" I asked. As an American, I question authority, especially when it comes from a male.

Although she was promised in marriage, it wasn't by her parents. It was done by an uncle, shortly after her birth. This was a custom in the Punjab province, but that was not where they were from. A marriage of a child was done to resolve feuds between different clans. The uncle was entrusted, through another uncle who was from Punjab, to resolve this feud. It went back decades, and when poor Fanta arrived on the scene he thought his problems were solved.

Fanta's uncle, her father's brother, had moved to the United States and became successful. He found a good-paying job and encouraged his brother and his family to join him. Arranging to pay the Deet, or money that would annul the contract, and wanting to protect their only daughter, they emigrated.

Fanta's brother, who was college-aged as well, returned to Pakistan to attend school and to habit the family property. He met a girl, which bothered his family. Not that he met a girl, but her clan believed in *Watta Satta*—if you want to marry off your son, you had better have a daughter to marry off in return. Once again, Fanta was in the middle.

"Do you have to? I mean, you're an adult now. You no longer even live there. Why would you have to marry an in-law?" I wondered.

"I don't, because the marriage must be consensual. My parents are against this family because they are not wealthy, and they want their daughter to marry my brother so all of them would be taken care of. They've already moved into our home there."

"How can they do that?"

"In reality they can't, but my brother won't stand up to them. They are forcing the marriage. My parents begged him to wait at least until they could arrive in December to be present, but her family wants it to happen next week."

This was mid-November. Thanksgiving break wasn't for another two weeks. Not that they were Americans or would celebrate as Americans do, but Fanta said it's a twenty-four-hour flight there . . . and I assume another twenty-four back . . . yeah, logistically this may not work to fly to Pakistan over the four-day Thanksgiving break.

While Pakistan is not known for women's rights or education, women do actually work. They are in the labor force. Does this mean they are working in offices as professionals? No. The majority of female labor can be found in rural areas, connected to agricultural production, raising livestock, and such. Fanta's family had high expectations for her and her two brothers.

Paula Evans

As is the custom in Pakistan, when the time came for her parents to arrange Fanta's marriage, they kept it close, as in betrothing her to a cousin. About a third of all marriages are to blood relatives, with preferences to first cousins.

Ewww, I thought, imagining my first cousins. *I'd abstain first. Oh, wait, I already do.*

Fanta was privileged enough to have spent her high school years in what I understood to be a religious, almost university of sorts where they studied the Koran. That was one of her dreams—to continue that education in a formal religious school. Becoming educated in the faith was prescribed by Muhammad. Islam encourages equality between the sexes as well as equality in education. This is different from the Pakistani view of women. Islamic women are encouraged to attend lectures and study sessions at mosques or wherever they may be held. Many even continue their education and earn graduate degrees. This practice began long before Americans really started to see the value of a college education for anyone, even men. In the mid-twentieth century, college was a way out of the draft during Vietnam. You didn't really need a higher education for most jobs at the time.

Shouldn't every religion encourage study of the basic tenants to which they allegedly espouse? Shouldn't every nation? This is probably why I laugh every time a study comes out that shows Americans are behind in some subject. The 'Muricans get all worked up about it, but in reality—we're into instant gratification. *What do you mean I have to, like, actually memorize something and write it down by hand? Can't I do it at home on my computer? Why do we need to learn math? I can't use my calcula-*

tor? That's not fair! And can I turn it in tomorrow? I know it's due today, but I didn't finish it. And why haven't you finished grading it? I gave it to you yesterday.

Fanta wanted to be a ulama.

"A llama?" I asked. A split second after saying that, her eyes blinked and I realized I said that out loud. "Do you mean like The Daily—I mean, Dalai Lama?"

Good one, Jane. Open mouth, insert foot. Did I just call the Dalai Lama "The Daily"? Damn that John Hughes, I thought, silently (at least I hope it was silent) cursing my CHU co-worker. He taught World History and the occasional Sociology class and loved reading international news stories. An avowed atheist, he especially loved stories about religious leaders like the pope and the Dalai Lama. He began referring to the Tibetan monk as "The Daily," because at this particular time there were nearly daily stories about his travels. That nickname stuck in my mind . . . and had just waltzed out of my mouth.

No, Fanta explained. A ulama is part of the religious elite of scholars at the top of the sectarian hierarchy.

I nodded very slowly. I understood, but I did not understand what I understood. My mind went back to *Fiddler on the Roof*— Tevye wanted to be one of the learned men reading seven hours every day. If he were a rich man . . .

Of course, my first thought is *Are they hiring? What does one do with that . . . job? Is it a job?*

It can be, she explained. *Why does my mind go into slow motion whenever I talk to her? Maybe it's to better understand her words through her accent? I feel like I go into a trance, with that sing-song voice, and the room is quiet . . .*

The ulama are thoroughly versed in the Muslim sciences (whatever that means), but from them come the religious teachers of the Islamic community. There is no priesthood in Islam, but the theologians, canon lawyers, judges and others come through these ranks. Or maybe they're trained by these ranks. But the point is they're mostly men.

"So how can you . . .? What do your parents think—"

She waved a hand as if shooing a fly. "Awwwn, it's not always all men. My parents are so worried about my brother right now, this gives them comfort. Did I tell you what his bride's family did . . ."

I listened, again, to her story (yes, she had told me what the family was doing—it was like my own personal soap opera here. *"Stay tuned for another episode of . . ."*) But I didn't understand. Maybe it was my narrow-mindedness brought about by a Midwestern upbringing, but weren't women second-class citizens? Weren't they treated and considered property? Weren't they treated brutally, without any rights?

"Sometimes," Fanta admitted. "But Muhammad was for equality. Women are equal in the Koran."

Have your fellow countrymen read that part? Really? Muhammad was for Women's Lib?

Women's Lib? Why yes, I did grow up in the 1970s, thank you for noticing.

Not all of the tribes treat women poorly, Fanta explained. In some cases, the women are even more emancipated than what we considered emancipated today by Western standards. Women do have and can have positions of power and authority. Her family belonged to such a tribe.

"But not my brother's future in-laws . . ." she started again.

When Islam began, women were treated poorly. Women had no rights. Everything the man had went to his sons after his death, not his wife. Muhammad instituted rights of property ownership, inheritance, education, and even divorce. This gave women certain basic safeguards. Muhammad made things better for women. "And this was back in the seventh century—when did the west give women such rights?" she asked, actually more demanded, in a proud sort of way. Muhammad wasn't the monster people think he was.

Fanta was a darling young woman and I was honored that she was entrusting me with her sorrows. The father was apoplectic, the mother was having heart palpitations, the uncle was spending late nights on the telephone (due to the time difference) trying to talk sense into the bride's family as well as his nephew. I found it fascinating—*Muslims are as screwed up as everyone else!*

They have the same problems with family, teenagers, in-laws—just like everyone in the west! I was learning a lot about the cultures (and some very specific differences between Indians and Pakistanis), but after a few heart-to-heart chats, it dawned on me.

I am giving advice to a person about marriage. Not her marriage, oh, no. Her brother's marriage, who is on a different continent. A marriage based on expectations from a family I don't even know. A marriage based on customs I do not even know, proclaimed by a prophet considered holy by several million people in the world. WWJD? What would Jesus do? Turn the other cheek? Wait—wrong parable.

What am I doing? Why am I doing it? How did I get into this situation? Why does this keep happening?

Because you are in a position of trust, you moron! My Mind screams at me. But was My Mind doing this at the time I was talking with Fanta? Heck, no! Why? Because My Mouth was speaking. My Mouth and My Mind are not connected. Never have been.

But isn't that dangerous? That they're not connected or that I'm giving advice?

Maybe it is dangerous, but . . . why not? I don't take my advice, why would I expect anyone else to?

Little did I know this was setting the theme for the next six months of my life.

Part II

Chapter 8

After the semester ended, I found I was missing the saga of Fanta's family. It was like my own personal soap opera. But I think I just missed having somewhere to go.

Winter in the Midwest isn't as much fun as you'd think. People dream of a White Christmas; we shudder at the thought. The beauty of a snow-covered landscape is indeed a wondrous sight. Add to it the gently falling snow in the moonlight, the silent effect it creates is absolutely sublime. But that's the stuff of movies. The gently falling snow is usually during rush hour, covering driveways and sidewalks that necessitate a 4 a.m. wake-up call to go out and shovel. So, for Midwesterners, any day that does not involve shoveling is a good one. Then there is the bitter cold. Some years we have a lot of it, some years not so much. One recent winter day, we had a forty-degree temperature spike—without ever hitting the freezing mark.

But out the door we go, to work, to church, to school, to wherever. Duty calls.

I never took much stock with the phenomenon known as SAD, seasonal affective disorder. People claim they need natural light or they go into a depression. Maybe it's because during daylight hours I'm usually in a windowless room that I don't really notice the lack of sunlight too much. But, judging from the behavior of others, everyone has more energy on a sunny day. Everyone seems happier.

But the melting snow reveals the mud. The brown grass. The dog poop. And everyone gets depressed again. Not to mention the slush and the black ice—*do you wear boots? Can you get by with sneakers? How waterproof are the sneakers? Do you wear sneakers and cover your stocking feet with plastic bags?*

And a funny thing I've noticed—everyone expects spring to hit the week after New Years. People tend to forget that winter began just before Christmas. Winter is great for Christmas, but then needs to give way to spring. It always reminds me of the title song to *Camelot*:

The winter is forbidden till December,
And exits March the second on the dot.

And don't get me started on the groundhog, which makes his appearance February the second on the dot. Either way you look at it (or how Punxsutawney Phil looks at it), spring is still six weeks away.

But this particular winter break was about par for the course. Not too much snow. The days were gray, but not storm-impending gray, just this side of "not sunny." The temps were in the twenties and thirties, which are easily bearable. In fact, the year Sophia and I went on our cruise and stopped in Stockholm, we visited a vodka bar. I'm not much of a drinker, but it was interesting. The vodka is served in "cups" made out of a block of ice. We were assigned parkas with thermal-insulated, vinyl-covered mittens to wear before we entered the official bar area.

Paula Evans

We were ordered (not merely encouraged) to zip up the parkas and put the hoods on because it was so brutally cold inside. It was thirty-five degrees Fahrenheit! Several of us who were from the Midwest looked at each other, flipped the hood back down and unzipped the jacket. Piece of cake.

Most educators will admit that any vacations they get they usually spend decompressing. Trying to get final projects and research papers graded and returned, getting grades calculated, and then trying to prepare for the family and the holidays do take a toll. The opportunity to vegetate cannot be overrated.

Having no family near me was both a blessing and a curse. I had nowhere to go, but I didn't really want to go anywhere. Everyone was always inviting me to Thanksgiving, but they were busy with their own families on Christmas. And this was my choice to be single—I had no one to blame but myself. But I really don't blame myself. As I've said, my life is what it is. I really don't believe I have any control over it and once I learned that I *do* have control over it, I realized I am woefully unequipped to exercise control.

The workplace friendships I've established—and this could be said for many people—don't really extend beyond the workplace. We're best of buds, we're inseparable while we're on the clock. But we're not the type of friends where you would go over to their house for coffee or call up and go to a movie. It's not that we didn't socialize outside of school, but it was usually going out for a meal almost immediately after our classes ended, while we were still in "school mode" and not "home mode."

And I'm okay with that. And if you make people truly think about this, they realize they don't socialize much outside of work. When people retire or quit for a new job, everyone shares contact information, swears allegiance to the end, but by Monday they're out of sight, out of mind. It's not intentional, it really just happens.

During this vacation from school, Anita and her family were in South America visiting her family, and Greta had dragged her family to Florida. This was the last year all her kids would be home, and by God, they were going to have a friggin' family vacation even though none of the children nor her husband wanted any part of it.

I got to the point I was predicting the type of day I would have by the first phone call of the day. I usually only received one phone call a day. But if by some miracle I received more than one, the first one set the tone for the day.

But this particular winter break fell into a definite pattern. I've never received so many phone calls in my life as I did during these three and a half weeks between semesters, and even for a few months following the break. The call would come about 10 a.m., out of respect for me, I guess, who was sleeping in. I was usually up by 9 a.m. so I could make some use of the day, even if it was just reading the paper, falling asleep halfway through, taking a ninety-minute nap before finishing it. Hey— why else do people read to fall asleep? I'm only obeying the law of nature, falling asleep while reading.

But the trend I noticed was that whoever called was the only call I received that day. They might have called two or three times during the day, but none of the others would call. The next day it might be a different person, or it may be the same person. But if Frank called first, I wouldn't hear from Greta,

Anita, or Fanta. If it was Anita, I wouldn't hear from Frank, Greta, or Fanta. And so on.

And why am I hearing from Frank?

Frank was my co-worker at Central Heights University. He taught math. He was the mystery man in our little adjunct office. It wasn't until he asked me to help his wife with her résumé and cover letter that I even knew he was married. He left CHU about a year before I started double-dipping at GNU. While we were on friendly terms (read: not adversarial) while we spent moments in the office, he had never called me at home. I didn't even know he had my phone number. He claims I gave it to him when I proofread his wife's résumé, in case she had questions. I never thought anything more about that gesture. *Note to self: Don't be so free to offer help!*

But again, why was Frank calling me? Especially a few days after Christmas.

After we exchanged greetings and my initial shock wore off . . . well, that's a lie. The initial shock segued into a larger shock.

Frank's wife had been working at the job I "helped" her get with my editing skills. He thanked me for my "genius" and command of the English language. She was rapidly advancing in her position.

"That's wonderful," I said, maybe a bit too enthusiastically.

"Well, I thought so as well until she went to China."

China! She is in China! Squeeee!

"That is so exciting!" I said, really enthusiastically. I'd love to go to China! My travel bug was still biting and needed to be scratched more.

I have no idea what he expected me to say. He was offended I was excited by his wife's trip to China. "How can you condone that?" he asked repeatedly. "They persecute Christians."

"Uh, okay."

"No," he said in very measured, pointed words, "that's not okay."

"But, Frank, it's China. As in not in Indiana China. If nothing else, she has bragging rights."

Wrong thing to say. Bragging is not what a good Christian woman does.

Okay, point taken. But still—it's China!! I had often considered trying to tag along on trips to China myself. Several area music groups often opened spots to allow people to travel with them on tours to foreign locales. I was in band in high school and technically, this was a band trip. Maybe I'm not the most talented person in the world (a massive understatement if I do say so myself), but I can hold my own. Kind of. I do have my moments. Well, *had* my moments. Past tense. But it's China! I could be a page turner, couldn't I? Schlep instruments to the auditorium? Something—just to be able to be part of a group traveling to China. That's not too much to ask, is it?

Frank then began talking about his children. His daughter was now twelve, his sons now high school age. They weren't adjusting well to their mother's absence. His daughter needed help.

Please, God—tell me this doesn't mean what I think it means. A twelve-year-old girl needing help usually means one thing—puberty hath struck. And from what little I know about men, I do know they're really not the ones a girl would want to talk to about this. And from what little I know about Frank, and he may be a wonderful and caring father, but . . . maybe I should get the guest room ready and just bring her home with me. Never mind the fact we've never met and we're total strangers, but I can only imagine what's going on in her head.

That's a lie—this is one situation where I would have no clue where to begin on anything going on in that child's head.

"Your daughter's not feeling well?" I gently tried to broach this subject while reaching with my foot, trying to grasp a kitchen chair and drag it to where I was standing with the phone. Yes, I still use land lines, and ones that are attached to a cord. What can I say? I'm a Luddite. *(You'll have to go look this one up yourself—it's worth the trip to the dictionary.)*

"I had to take her to the emergency room last night . . ."

My mind began to race before he finished the statement. *Shit—it is what I think it is!!!*

"The ER?" I asked, trying to not let my panic come through my voice.

"Yes," he replied, slightly exasperated that he had to repeat what he just said. "The doctors said it was most likely anxiety—"

What? Anxiety?? I'm no doctor, but I'm pretty sure anxiety doesn't cause periods—wait—it's probably the panic once it set in. Shitshitshit.

"Anxiety?" My voice began to rise in panic.

"Yes, anxiety from missing her mother."

I obviously missed something in translation. I tried to piece together what I thought Frank said and repeated it back to him. "You took her to the ER because she missed her mother?"

Frank became more exasperated. "No, I took her to the ER because she was hyperventilating—she was having a panic attack because she missed her mother. My sons are also missing her terribly."

"Okay, so they're physically fine, no one's bleeding or anything *(damn, bad choice of words)* but just this is new for them?"

"Right. My wife has never traveled without the children. This is their first time really being separated from her."

My own hyperventilating was easing. So no one's bleeding, they just miss their mother. And probably panicked because Mr. Mom here—wait a sec.

And under the heading that my brain and mouth are not connected, I hear this voice coming out of my mouth:

"So, no one's bleeding, right?"

"Right."

Thank God. Thank God he didn't pick up on that reference. And thank God I never had kids, so I never have to have this discussion with another human being.

"Could it be you're just resentful of being left with the kids?"

WTF did I just say?!

There was a moment of silence on the other end. I could see his mustache and right eye twitching from here. No matter how minor a discomfort, his facial muscles began to twitch before he answered.

"No, I'm not resentful. The kids are old enough to know to do their chores while I work in my office."

He resents it—he's locking himself away.

"It's just that a mother's duty to her children doesn't involve her traveling overseas for two weeks."

Oink.

"Well," I began, "the world is changing. Women are expected to work these days and travel is part of the deal. Your daughter is learning a life lesson to better prepare her, and your sons are learning to be more understanding about their wives' careers in the future."

Frank sighed. He got off his chest what he needed to say, he claimed he was feeling better about the situation, but he wasn't convincing. Was he that chauvinistic that he truly expected his wife home to cook three meals a day and take care of their children so he didn't have to? He claims not, but you can't always teach an old dog a new trick. We ended the conversation and I didn't really think anything more about it.

Until his next call a few days later.

Frank gave me an update. The children were adjusting better and, I'm sure, shipping them off to Grandma and Grandpa's for a few days didn't hurt any of them. He was still . . ."obsessed". . . about his wife's business trip to China.

"Do you know what else? She didn't even take her Bible with!"

Wow—this came out of left field. If she's in a hotel, what's the problem? I'm sure the Gideons would have been there by now. I don't travel much, but it seems like every hotel I've stayed at there was a Bible there, courtesy of the Gideons. But then again, China is

Communist, so maybe the Gideons hadn't been there. Again, Frank, what's the problem?

He then related the story of their discussion about the opportunity for taking this trip, and the implications of leaving her Bible home *(was it an oversight? No, this was deliberate, he insisted)* and what the Communists did and did not do or believe. They were persecuting Christians—a sign of the end times.

Okay, I had to give him that. I had been seeing accounts in the news of what Chinese and North Koreans were doing to Christians. One particularly nasty story involved the Communists having Christians prostrate while a steam roller was driven over their heads.

"Before they left, each person was given a list of things to pack and not pack," Frank explained, laying out his evidence like a prosecuting attorney. "They were told not to bring a Bible, but if they must, the government must register it and there were forms to fill out. And when they leave China, they again must be questioned and the Bible they brought must be in their possession."

"Why?"

"To make sure Christians aren't leaving them behind for the Chinese to read—it's illegal. The Chinese don't want their people becoming Christians."

Something isn't adding up. If they both agreed she would take her Bible—*why am I even having this discussion?*—that could be open defiance of the wife to the husband. Or not. Maybe she was being overly conscious of the Chinese culture? Maybe she was trying to avoid delaying the group by having to register the Bible and fill out a lot of forms, and opted to not even have it in her possession. It would save time and effort. Judging from Frank's behavior, I have a feeling he is considering this "open defiance." *Oink.*

Is this really what married couples talk about? I've never been married. I've never really been around men, so I don't know how or what they think, or even if they're capable of thought. I don't know what married women think or how or if they even do. The married women I know are either too independent or too stupid to form their own coherent thoughts. Again, granted, I am ignorant on the subject of marriage, but everything you see on TV or in movies is of couples arguing about bills and in-laws, not about reading the Bible. I mean, what do most movies about married couples deal with? Infidelity?

Oh, no, not that . . .

Frank was also convinced that his wife's boss, Benji, was only doing this trip to pad his résumé. *Taking a business trip to China is padding his résumé?*

Benji apparently saw a business opportunity in China. His company could expand its base overseas, and Benji and a few others were there making connections to possibly further the company's reach into other countries. I had no idea what Benji's company made, but there were parts needed and somehow China could provide them.

It's unethical, Frank insisted. *How so?* "Benji is not that smart to see such an opportunity."

Okay, I can accept that. He may not be, but he has my vote. I know less about business than I do about marriage, so if he sees an opportunity, who am I to question. *So? What's the point, Frank?*

Frank went into weasel mode. "I need someone (read: me) to search the internet for stories and . . . to prove that he's lying."

Oh, good God. You're asking me, the self-proclaimed Luddite, to do internet research on a topic I know nothing about to prove someone I don't know is lying about "something."

And damn me if I didn't do it. I really need to get a life.

Chapter 9

Despite the distance, there was an occasional call from Anita, who was visiting her family in Brazil, and from Greta, who was with her family in Florida. These calls surprised me almost as much as Frank's calls. *You're in an exotic locale with your loved ones—why the heck are you calling me?*

Their husbands would be in a shop or taking a shower or somewhere where they had just a few moments to vent. They would use practically every second to tell me, very rapidly, about what was going on. Anita called twice from Brazil over that two-week period. The calls were so brief I almost forgot she had called. She was very chatty and spoke very fast. I thought it a bit odd, but didn't think more about it until that next summer. Although I didn't realize it at the time, looking back, her calls made a lot of sense.

For poor Greta, the family vacation wasn't a dream come true, it was more of a nightmare. Her eldest child was rebelling because he wanted to be home with his friends before they all left for college next fall. The oldest daughter was going through the angsts of puberty and rebellion, because she could only text her friends and not go to their houses. The younger two were upset because they weren't spending every waking moment at Disney World.

She was used to dealing with the kids and their "petty little problems." What an odd term for Greta to use. She was a great mother. She loved her children. She loved their growing and maturing process no matter how frustrating. I have never heard her say that word—frustrating—or any other word or term that would indicate displeasure with her children.

And this is probably why I don't have kids—I can barely tolerate adult behavior let alone kids trying to learn things.

With each of the calls, after their venting, there would be a deep breath and the innocuous question to me, "So, how are you doing?"

What? Uh, is it my turn to talk? Crap. What is going on with me?

This was winter break from school—I had nowhere to go, and half the time wasn't even getting out of my pajamas. Nothing much goes on between the holidays. It's winter in Indiana. I'm either shoveling snow or dying of boredom, counting the hours to the next meal.

Who am I kidding? Counting hours? Hahahahah. I crack myself up. Eating anything not nailed down as my mood dictated is more like it.

I couldn't understand why Anita would call me, of all people. Aside from the sheer expense ("Oh, it's not that expensive," she would say in that thick German accent—I guess not if you and your husband were each pulling in a hundred grand a year), she was with family! She was seeing both of her parents each day. Granted, they were divorced, but . . . why not talk to them?

"Ah, they don't know anything," she said. "I'd rather talk to you."

I am flattered, but the parents were each two marriages ahead of me.

I began to realize maybe the calls from Greta and Anita wasn't so much the need for advice, but just a chance to get their thoughts right in their own heads. Sometimes when you force yourself to verbalize your thoughts, when you really focus on finding the right words, you see the solution and end up solving the problem yourself.

But that wasn't happening with Greta. Or Frank. Anita was much smarter than me and would come up with some off-the-wall connection that she saw but I couldn't, even after she told me how she came to that conclusion.

But they all wanted to know what I thought. What did I see that they weren't seeing? They weren't asking this outright, but the conversations were always going in that direction.

What do I do? they'd ask.

I have no idea.

This dawned on me after Greta's second call a few days later.

Her husband and son stormed out of their rented condo before breakfast this particular day. Her daughter was in the shower and the other two were in their shared bedroom, having a tantrum. Poor Greta was at her wits' end. She relayed the events of the morning to me. From what I could deduce, it wasn't the kids and their "petty little problems," it was her husband who was the big problem. He traveled quite a bit for his job, so to have all of them together in one location for more than forty-eight hours was proving a challenge. The kids loved having him there, but they weren't used to his strictness and he wasn't used to their "petty little problems."

This explains her frustration and where she came up with that term.

She so wanted a wonderful vacation for her children, to have these memories as they grow and begin their own families. She planned an adventure for the whole family, each day to do something each person would love—petting and swimming with dolphins for the one, hanging out on the beach for another, renting a boat and fishing for her husband, a day at Disney World to get pictures of her little princesses with the real princesses.

But nothing for her?

"Oh, I enjoy all of this. There really isn't anything specific that I need to do," she explained.

All she wanted was a wonderful time as a family. "Is that too much to ask?" she nearly choked back a sob on the other end of the phone. "What do I do?"

Damned if I know.

Well, that's not true. I know what I would do. But then again, I'm not living that life, with those circumstances. I tend to focus only on myself. I don't mean for that to sound selfish, but I am the only one I need to worry about. After my mother's death, my responsibility for another person ended. So, consideration for the feelings of another person was more at the level of friendship maintenance. Greta's husband would insist on doing something that the other family members were not comfortable with or happy about. *So why not just tell him?* Yes, direct communication is the best—everyone says so. But . . . but . . . when it's you doing it, that's a very scary prospect. Especially for the children—do you disrespect your father to be honest? It's easier to complain to mom—she can smooth things over and deal with dad.

I know when I am in similar circumstances I will lie through my teeth to avoid a direct confrontation. This direct, honest communication all sounds good in theory. *Stand up for yourself—put yourself first!* What else do you want to know? I've got millions of ideas.

Except when it comes to standing up for *myself* . . . that's as foreign a concept to me as marriage.

Physician, heal thyself.

Chapter 10

Frank was becoming a pest.

This was his third phone call this week. I wasn't sure if he just needed a shoulder to cry on or wanted someone to vent to. What do men do? This is the closest I've ever come to having a relationship with a man, so to say I was out of my league was a massive understatement. I have no clue about marriage, and I certainly have no insight from the male point of view. On anything.

Are you jealous your wife is on a trip? I asked.

No, he wasn't.

Are you jealous of the boss?

No, he claimed. The no-talent son-of-a-bitch couldn't hold a candle to him, workwise.

Did he just say son-of-a-bitch? WTF. He's never said a negative word about anyone, even when we were sharing the office with thrice-divorced John and his hare-brained theories about women! Even when we all were griping about what a jerk John was when he wasn't in the room, Frank would keep out of the discussion.

So what's the problem? Do you resent being left home with the kids?

He claimed no, but I kind of suspected he did. Other than the occasional comment that he would play a game of catch in the backyard, he never mentioned his kids.

He did, however, resent the cost of the trip.

Really? The company isn't paying for it?

Yes, but there was the cost of the passport, transportation to the airport, money for extras . . .

Are you that cheap? Or poor? Or jealous?

That struck a nerve. I think I'm onto something.

"What do I do?" Frank kept asking me.

Damned if I know.

How deep do I pry? Even to make a half-assed guess I would need details. I really knew nothing about his wife. We had never met. I didn't even know her first name. You'd never know he was married—no ring, no photos, no mention of his private life. Then again, with children, how much do you reveal?

Finally, I suggested he talk to his minister. Frank was very religious. He wasn't a Bible thumper or "Praise the Lawd" type of guy; he was a good man. Never cursed, never gossiped, wouldn't even hug another woman. I discovered this and went out of my way to hug him, more to just piss him off. That's the way I am. I'm miserable, and misery loves company.

The minister made sense to me. If he was so angry about his wife leaving her Bible at home, they obviously had to have a minister who knew the family. And if this was about possible infidelity, for the love of God keep me out of it! Er, I mean, a minister could provide proper marriage counseling, something a mere mortal could not.

Especially one who had never been married.

Advice For The Lovelorn Pakistani

That advice he did take. His final call was the next week when he let me know that he did call his minister and would be speaking with him later that week.

Now I can go back to my ninety-minute naps while reading the newspaper.

Boy, I sure cannot wait for school to start!

Chapter 11

When I first met Sophia, she gave me a book she loved, titled *Women who Run with the Wolves*. She read it and had purchased several copies which she was giving to the women in her life, me included. I was honored to be part of such an august group. I greatly admired Sophia and wanted to drink from her fountain of knowledge and soak it all in. So I devoured the book (as much as a very slow reader can devour anything).

I didn't fully get it.

I was in my late twenties, living with my mother, still basically a little girl. I was too immature to fully appreciate or even understand most of the concepts discussed in the book.

The stories were about women, whom the author felt was an endangered species. Using some fairy tales and myths, she would show that (in my opinion) women are strong and we weren't being recognized as such. We had bought society's line that men were in charge, men were gods, etc. But, as I remember it, women were just as good as men, definitely thinking in different ways, but often almost smarter than men. We needed to reach deep inside of us to bring that fierceness, our inner wolf, out again.

Advice For The Lovelorn Pakistani

Now, my problem was, I didn't think of myself as a "woman." I was never really a girly girl. I didn't wear makeup, I mowed the lawn, I got dirty, I could change a tire, I had my own tool box (a gift from my mother, no less—actually, she gave me two of them over the years). I wasn't a princess waiting for rescue. I was more of the schmuck doing the rescuing because the men were too stupid to step up until the last minute, after *I* had cleared the path for them to take all the credit.

So, reaching down into a soul, yearning for power, things like that—no, that wasn't me. I was working two jobs and going to grad school and living daily with the demoralizing ridiculing that my mother considered conversation. I was living life day by day, trying not to kill someone, just enduring until I could go to sleep and then get up the next day and start the ordeal again. I remember a parody copy of my college newspaper which repeatedly said, "Life's a bitch, and then you die." It became painfully clear that the editor was a very stressed-out senior, but it was a mantra that could not be denied.

Life is a bitch, and then you die.

And when you live with a bitch, death can't come soon enough.

As much as I desperately needed the advice and guidance in the book, it was more of a thought kept in the back of my mind rather than a daily mantra.

So this was just another one of those things that affect everyone else but not me. There were a lot of those things, and they rolled off my back like water off a duck. So, years later, after my mother's death and my move, when Sophia gave me a copy of *The Secret*, I did read it. I was . . . well, I'm not sure if fascinated is the correct word. Intrigued? Mildly interested? That's it! I was mildly interested in it because Sophia was. I admired her life—she would plan things and they came true. In fact, shortly after she gave me the book, she was going to be leaving for a sabbatical in Europe for several months! Talk about a dream come true. So, if Sophia likes the book, I need to look into it.

I began to read it, and it was innocuous enough. It made a lot of sense. But I read a passage, and what it said I have no idea. Even after re-reading the book, I don't recognize the passage, but it shook me to the core. What I read, I interpreted it as basically I need to be aware of messages being sent to me and this particular weekend was full of messages of "We don't want you."

Now, I'm the proverbial straw that broke the camel's back. I'm probably hypersensitive to people's reactions and comments. Maybe in my desperate need to be loved and accepted I will often blame myself even though I know I am not to blame. So this interpretation just shook me to the core.

I did think about it for a few days. And I realized I was guilty of what I accused others of—taking things out of context. So I began the book again and finished it.

It never said I "was not wanted." Just the opposite—if you think you are not wanted, then you won't be. And, in all honesty, I was living proof of *The Secret*. I had two specific instances where things weren't going right (not that things ever did go right, but these two stood out) and I asked myself mentally, "What else can go wrong?"

Within moments, I found out.

Advice For The Lovelorn Pakistani

Like the time when I decided to wear these big, clunky sandals all summer. I loved those sandals. Then, for the first day of the new semester at CHU, I decided to wear my blue Hush Puppies with a nice dress. I rarely had occasion to wear them as it was, but I did finally have an outfit that wouldn't clash with the blue shoes. And, oh, my, were they comfortable. Except this day.

The night before, I could not fall asleep. I don't know if it was nerves or excitement, but I swear I did not get more than an hour of sleep that night. The next day was gray and rainy, but I was going to wear that dress and those blue Hush Puppies. My class began at 8 a.m. which meant I had to be on the road by seven, partly due to the distance and traffic, but also because I did not go to the orientation session the week before to get the classroom keys and mailbox combination. So I had to take care of some business, but that wasn't a big deal—the classroom doors were never locked and I had plenty of time between my classes to get all of that paperwork stuff done. Not a problem.

The fifteen-foot walk from the front door of my house to my car was one of the longest of my life. The Hush Puppies had apparently shrunk since the last time I wore them—before my summer of clunky sandals? Oh, man, my feet spread out over the nice, wide platform of those sandals so now I couldn't fit into the dress shoes. Of course, I didn't think about this until half way through the commute. And it wouldn't have done much good to have brought another pair of shoes, because if these didn't fit, none of my others would have either.

Except the big, clunky sandals.

Since I didn't go to the orientation, I didn't have the required parking permit, so I had to park in "Lot 7," which was at least a quarter mile from the campus. Central Heights University was a small campus, consisting of only three buildings with a fourth under construction, and this lot, at the edge of the property, was not paved. It had rocks, as opposed to gravel, and it was sufficient.

For parking cars, not walking, in the rain, in my very tight, blue Hush Puppies.

After what seemed an eternity I entered the department office to get the classroom roster and other papers needed to begin the semester. The department chairman, almost as if on cue, rushed out of his office shouting, "It's about time you got here!"

I looked at the secretary, who was seated behind a counter behind me. *Was he talking to me?*

I looked at my watch—I had plenty of time to get to the other building for my class. The chairman continued talking. "My son is in your class."

I looked at him, then flipped through the roster. He had a common surname so I would not have known if this student was his child or not. "Steven?" I said. He nodded.

Fuck.

So off I clomped down the hallway, down the stairs, out into the gray drizzle, to the next building, up the stairs and saw the crowd of students outside of a classroom. My classroom.

"The door's locked," one young man said.

I grabbed the handle in disbelief. "Since when do they lock the doors here?" I asked.

I noticed a telephone in the hallway and obediently "pressed 0 for campus police." *Can't wait for Junior to tell his father about this.* What a day. And it was only 8:01.

Campus security showed up and unlocked the door, lecturing me in front of the students about the importance of keeping the doors locked. "Where is your key?" he demanded.

"I haven't picked it up yet—I've never known the doors to be locked."

"Well, make sure you get one."

I looked at him, wishing this humiliation would end. "I intend to, just after this class is finished."

I'm going to be fired. I knew it. Junior was going to tell Daddy how incompetent I am and about the cop and how we started late, and I just knew this was my last day on campus. I looked around at the students, trying to figure out which one was Steven. I gave my opening spiel.

CHU insisted that students refer to you as professor, unless you had a doctorate degree, then you were Dr. Whomever. It always reminded me of that scene in *The Music Man* where Harold Hill keeps trying to get Marian the Librarian's attention during the ice cream social. "Professor? Of what? At what university do they give a degree . . ."

That scene *always* went through my head every time I said the word or was called Professor Smith. Then there was the husband of a friend who burst out laughing and said, "You play piano?"

What?

"Professor. That's what they call the piano players in the whorehouses!"

Totally humiliated, my mouth began to speak. My brain and mouth aren't connected, so comebacks come faster than they probably should. And, of course, timing is everything.

I arched an eyebrow. "And how would you know that?"

This got everyone to laugh, especially his wife sitting next to him. "Hey—yeah, how do *you* know that?" she asked.

But this particular morning, the other part of my problem is that, with Junior Department Head in my class, I probably shouldn't use my standard joke. "Good morning. My name is Professor Smith and to make sure you are in the right class, this is advanced nuclear physics."

Only a few people would catch that. I was teaching English Composition 101.

I love college students—the first day they are scared to death.

So I began to take attendance, eyeing the male students to see which one was Steven. I really wish I didn't know to whom he was related.

As each of the white males responded, I realized there were only three males left: one white, one black, one Asian.

Steven was the Asian kid. *Was he adopted?* Because his father was white. From somewhere in the back of my mind, I recalled a tidbit of gossip—Mrs. Department Chair was Korean.

I got through the class relatively unscathed. As soon as the class ended I had to go to the campus police department to pick up my official key so I could get into the classrooms. I had a ninety-minute break between classes, and each class was in a different building. And, the "office" that was shared by all adjuncts? The basement of the *third* campus building (no elevator access). Ah, the joys of college teaching. I need to charge mileage.

While the campus is small, it is "hilly." And by hilly, keep in mind this is the Midwest. We're flat. Highway viaducts were sledding hills to us—the only elevated surfaces around. The campus police department was down a hill. It wasn't like it was a big hill, but keep in mind I am wearing my very-tight, blue Hush Puppies and it is raining. I'm a natural-born klutz (it's a gift!) and new shoes on wet asphalt is never a good combination. But I did make it to the building in under ten minutes—it was 8:56.

They opened at 9 a.m.

What else could go wrong?

The walk back, that's what. Now I was traveling *up*hill. Suddenly, this little hill has turned into the Matterhorn. I ended up walking on the wet, muddy grass so at least I could get some traction. This was going to be a very long day.

By the time I got to my next class, I looked like a drowned rat (no offense to rats meant). The key didn't work. Apparently, there is a "trick" to this particular room. We finally got in, I began to take roll, and once again thought, "What else could go wrong?"

I turned to see the director of the Composition Program standing in the doorway, camera to her eye, pointed at me. Now, this is the lady who hired me to teach composition in the first place.

"Take that photo and I will kill you," I said, in front of the students. *Just batting a thousand here, aren't I?* I'm just determined to be fired.

She smiled. "I'm just taking photos for our web page. We wanted to get actual students and professors in action."

I looked at her and then she noticed my rain-soaked-and-air-dried hair. I really wasn't the best poster child to put out on the World Wide Web.

I pointed to the left. "There are the students. Go for it."

By the time the class ended, and I emerged from the windowless classroom, the sky was beginning to brighten. By the time I got to the car, the sun was beginning to peek from behind the clouds. I vowed that as soon as I got home I was putting the Hush Puppies back in the box, never to be worn again without training the feet to be enclosed in tight spaces. Note to self for the next summer.

I was reminded of this day while reading *The Secret*. The Law of Attraction—if you think of negative things, you attract them to you. Dale Carnegie was right—The Power of Positive Thinking. Each time I thought *What else could go wrong?*, I immediately found out.

Right then and there I swore I would *never* again ask what else could go wrong. Until the next time.

Chapter 12

Maybe it was the new year, with its infinite possibilities, or maybe it was reading *The Secret* and about all the chances of "attracting what you want in life," and maybe it was all the conversations with Frank about "talking to your minister," but I began to find myself also wanting a fresh start.

I knew I wasn't happy, I knew I didn't know why or how to fix it.

But after my mother's death, I decided to move out of my childhood home. When I actually was able to think about me and my feelings, I knew something was missing from my soul. And this was odd because I really didn't know what a soul was. As with everything, it was something other people had but I didn't. I needed a peaceful feeling. Where do I even begin to look for it? *Well, nothing else is working, so let's try a church!*

It wasn't that I was missing my mother; no, not at all. So that wasn't the problem. But there was no peace in my soul. It had been many years since I attended church. I didn't come from a family of churchgoers. My mother insisted I know the 23rd Psalm and the Lord's Prayer and that was all I really needed to know. That's what her grandmother taught her, and grandma was very religious. So that was all I needed. I did go to church during my elementary school years with friends—more just to get out of the house—but I was ordered not to bring it home. She didn't care and didn't want to hear about religion. As far as she was concerned, she was God and the sooner I accepted it the better.

When you have a parent who thinks she's God, Satan becomes a wonderful option. I'm sure he would be much nicer.

Despite the day-to-day drudgery of caring for and just living with an elderly parent, I was totally convinced I would die first, and I even felt horribly guilty because who would take care of my mother when I was gone? No one could put up with her even in the best of situations. She was a drama queen—*I will feel this way, you may not. I am the victim, you're just a lazy, self-centered bitch.* She may have switched the words occasionally, but often did not.

And really? I'm a lazy, self-centered bitch? Have we looked in the mirror lately?

But something Frank had said just struck me at my core, because I don't think I have ever heard anyone say that phrase before. I've known many people who were regular churchgoers. I've known many who were religious and faithful. I've known more than a few Bible-thumpers. But I had never met anyone who actually declared: I'm a Christian.

I don't know why that struck me as odd and stayed buried in my subconscious. People always profess to be a Christian but don't act like one. This was just so matter-of-fact. When I returned home one day, I saw the tell-tale pamphlets from the local Jehovah's Witnesses: *Alive!* and *Watchtower*. The cover story on *Watchtower* was about Moses and forgiveness. It was kind of an odd combination, Moses and forgiveness (I mean, this wasn't in *The Ten Commandments*, after all. Yul Brynner didn't forgive Charlton Heston for anything.) and, feeling more than a little down and depressed this particular day, I decided to read the article. Followers of *The Secret* would say I attracted this article and, *Twilight Zone* theme aside, I could probably agree and admit I needed to see these words at this specific time.

Basically, the article told the story about Moses, and the problems the ancient Israelites gave Moses for leading them out of Egypt. He could have easily just left them to rot, or taken them back to Egypt, but he didn't. So even though you may be hurt, that pain doesn't last. Get over it. God will provide strength, but basically, don't let the turkeys get you down. Do the right thing and it will all work out in the end.

Maybe there was something to this religion thing after all.

But Frank's statement haunted me: I am a Christian. I learned I needed the belongingness that comes with being part of a community. Did it matter which community? A church as opposed to a municipality? No. Either one is a community. Po-tay-toe, Po-tah-toe, as they say.

After the trauma of moving into a new home in the middle of a flood, I figured the time was right to begin attending church. But which one? I started with the local Kingdom Hall—there actually was one in my new town! After reading about Moses and the hurt, I figured it was as good a place to start as any. I had attended a few meetings of the Jehovah's Witnesses before (wouldn't you know, I got the one kid who came back and insisted on giving a Bible study). They were nice people. All were very polite and respectful of every single person in attendance. They weren't even freaked out when I attended, being the token white. Conversely, when I went to another hall to hear a co-worker give the weekly "talk," that all-black congregation flipped out. Well, flipped out is a slight exaggeration, but I wasn't expected and really wasn't wanted until his wife, whom I had never met, mind you, came up and gave me a hug. Of course, I had to be there to support Antwon and hear his talk. I've worked with this guy for twelve years and never heard him say a dozen words total. To hear him give a talk and speak for forty-five minutes straight? You better believe I'm watching this.

You never heard a cough during their public talks. No rustling of papers, no squirming kids. They are altogether a different breed. And I have to admit, even though I didn't agree with everything they said, I did always feel better afterward. Maybe a little lighter in spirit? But I was somehow changed. So I figured this new Kingdom Hall experience would be about the same.

It wasn't.

They were nice enough people, but rather than feeling uplifted and consoled I was darn near suicidal. Was it me? Or them? This is not at all what I needed. I already felt crappy—I didn't need to continue this feeling with a church.

I decided to try a Lutheran church, because I had traveled past this church at least twice a day every day. I figured close enough: I had graduated from a Lutheran university, and who knows? I was baptized a Baptist. I'm an equal-opportunity offender.

Advice For The Lovelorn Pakistani

Not exactly the friendliest group of people. I'm not a social butterfly. I admit it: I'm pretty antisocial. But this group had me beat.

Just by luck, one Thursday evening I was driving home and noticed a lighted sign for a church. They had Saturday night services. And this one particular week I needed . . . something. I decided to try it out come Saturday night.

The red brick building was small, but adequate. There was a short wing with classrooms, two on each side. There was a lobby area the width of the church, with several clusters of chairs and some tables which look like they came from someone's office reception area. One thing that struck me was the racks and stacks of brochures and reading materials, even one for the local cemetery. *Really? Who advertises cemeteries? And—wait a second—this is where my great-grandparents are buried.* I took the pamphlet with. I was in no mood to battle mentally with anyone or anything.

As an observer, this first service was all right. The people weren't standoffish or overly friendly. The minister was all right. I guess he could grow on a person. Something he said in the sermon struck me:

"Don't make snap decisions, especially with regard to your faith. Take the time to understand what you are feeling. When you decided to join this church, you may have taken the time to talk with people. Don't base your decisions on individual personalities, because we are not all alike. Somedays we may be feeling out of sorts and be overly critical, and other days we may be in a happier mood where we agree with everything. As Jesus told us to forgive seventy times seven, keep your hearts open to a second chance, or a third, or a fourth . . . however many is needed."

Hmm, it's almost like he's speaking directly to me. Maybe I was too critical of the last two church visits. Maybe I need to give this church thing another try. Maybe I will come back here next week.

This was a Lutheran church, but they said they were LCMS. Maybe that was a bigger question I needed to ask.

"What does that mean?" I asked.

"We're a Lutheran Church Misery Synod," one older woman replied to my inquiry.

Misery Synod? Like Stephen King's Misery? *What—are you guys snake handlers? Or do you sacrifice virgins? I'm a newcomer and a virgin, aren't I? This can't possibly go well for me.*

I took home some brochures, including the one for the local cemetery, the one where my great-grandparents are buried. *Odd*, I thought, *why would they be advertising a cemetery? Do they get kickbacks for their sacrifices?*

I began reading the cemetery brochure first. Even though I had never met my great-grandparents, and from all accounts I heard from relatives they were very religious, I couldn't fathom what connection they would have with this ankle-breaking, Cujo-worshipping cult of snake handlers.

"To be buried in Concordia," the brochure explained, "a person must belong to one of the eight following Lutheran Churches-Missouri Synod."

Missouri?

Come to think of it, that woman did have a touch of a twang. So—I'm just guessing here—maybe she was saying "Missouri" and I was hearing "Misery?"

Advice For The Lovelorn Pakistani

Then it dawned on me—*how did Grandma get buried out there? Did she attend one of the eight churches?*

One of my mother's cousins did a pretty extensive family tree, even tracing each dead person to their funeral program, the hymns sung and Bible verses recited. I was interested in genealogy and was the keeper of the information. But my interest began some 25 years ago when I thought I would have descendants with whom to share this information. I found the genealogy and flipped the pages until I got to my great-grandparents. Her listing, more than a half-century after her death, put her right in the middle of the list. A lot of predecessors and a lot of progeny.

The cousin had everything listed, including the church name (one of the eight!) and the number of burial in Concordia.

Seriously? The number of burial in the cemetery?

As I said, she did extensive research.

As I looked over the pages, at people long dead and gone and not even a blip on my radar, I found many were also buried in Concordia. And then it dawned on me.

Holy shit, we're Lutheran!

I swear, nobody tells me anything.

But I found that the Cujo worshippers were in actuality a very nice group of people and welcomed me as one of their own. It was a wonderful feeling, actually filling that void I had in my, for lack of a better term, soul. Occasionally, a few would ask amongst themselves, "Where on earth did she come from?" But no one bothered to ask me.

Not that my past is a secret, but . . . it's not that important to me. I had moved to this town to get away from my past and that really wasn't important now. Did it make a difference who I was or where I'm from? I don't want to relive it. Not that my background was bad, but I'm not exactly proud of it. How do you explain to people about the characters you met as a child as a place holder in line for your mother in the welfare office waiting to pick up food stamps? Most of these people were Republicans, wealthy (in my opinion), grew up in two-parent families and raised their children with the person they married and with whom they had these children. In my family, I need a scorecard of how everyone is related and to whom. I can't explain it to people because they just can't fathom it.

But one evening, I had an epiphany. The youth group was trying to raise funds to attend a mission conference. I could direct a show using them, they could sell tickets, I could get the directing bug out of my system, and it would be a win-win.

And where on earth did this directing bug come from? One of the English professors at GNU U also taught theatre. By way of introduction and welcome to Great Northern, I ended up being forcibly volunteered to help him with the student production. I didn't do much to help, but I did get to observe him work a few scenes and thought that would be something I would like to try. So, a simple thing with kids, controlled experience—I could probably do that.

Ironically, the sermon that night dealt with "using your talents." After the sermon, I asked to speak to the pastor. He was a fairly young man, barely thirty, with short, dark hair and a goatee that would appear and then disappear about a month later. The youth group was a special source of pride to him—he helped create it at this church. So the importance of supporting the group was not lost on anyone in the congregation. And as it takes a village to raise a child, this church was that village.

"Funny you should mention using your talents in the sermon this evening," I said. "I was thinking of offering my services to help the youth group raise money. I would like to direct a play and I could use the kids. This could be a fund raiser for them."

His eyes lit up. "Could you direct a Christmas show?"

I shrugged my shoulders. "Sure." I knew I was going to regret this, but what the heck. He became more animated and excited.

"And for Easter?"

"Uh, sure." I had never heard of an Easter show before, but what the heck? I didn't know much about churches.

His eyes were sparkling, and he was smiling, shifting his weight on both feet. "Can you direct a choir?"

"Uh," *could I?* I remember in sixth grade music class we had to learn conducting in 2/4, 3/4 and 4/4 time. I still remembered that. "Probably," I lied.

As I left, I realized that he was downright giddy. People aren't giddy anymore. I don't think I've ever seen anyone who was actually giddy. Is that word even part of the lexicon anymore? Something's rotten in Denmark, I feared.

Two weeks later, I discovered why the pastor was so giddy. His sermon that week was a plea for assistance from the congregation because Eunice, the woman who single-handedly ran the Sunday School Program, as well as directed the Christmas programs, was moving downstate and, as this was mid-October, there was no one to take on the Christmas program.

Now, I hate being set up. And I walked right into this one. *Thanks a lot, God.*

As I was new to church and didn't know any of the children, I began visiting the classes during Sunday School to listen to the children read. The shows were very simple—there were no auditions, no rehearsals during the week. The shows were pretty much already written for all of the LCMS churches and could be downloaded off a web site for free. The shows basically consisted of putting kids in costumes and having them read from a script. Very simple, no muss or fuss.

Costumes?

Yes, this church actually had some very nice costumes, in storage. Many years ago, one mother, who made her own children's clothing, decided to make very elaborate Wise Men costumes for her son and his friends, so they could be the three kings. The crowns were bejeweled, the smocks had gold trim and a few jewels on them. There were about a dozen various shepherd costumes and about two dozen "angel" costumes (basically, white polyester ponchos and gold Christmas tree garland pinned in a circle on the little heads). It was a ritual with the kids, having grown up with it ever since they began preschool Sunday School classes. The boys knew they "made it" when they got to wear the Wise Men costumes.

The preschoolers had their own costumes—they were all sheep. Pillowcases with big black circles, representing the curly wool, were pulled over their clothes and white knit caps, with black felt ears on each side, were pulled over their heads. Their big scene, also an annual tradition, was singing "Away in a Manger." It stole the show every year. They only knew the one verse, and you could barely see them from the back, but the entire church loved it.

So, for a first experience, this was simple enough. It wasn't broke, so no need to fix it.

After a few years, I found myself volunteering to teach Sunday School. *I know, I know—I walked right into that one as well.* But my sole purpose (no pun intended) was to do my casting for the show throughout the year, see which kids were regular attendees and could read well. I was feeling more and more at home with these people, this new family. After about a year, I decided to become a Lutheran. Once I did that, I became more active with the church. For once, I felt wanted. It's a really nice feeling.

During my spring break, the women at church knew I was free and invited me to join them in preparing for Holy Week.

Now, I didn't mind doing this. Nor did I see the big red cape being waved at me. Excuse me while I charge headlong into *this* situation . . .

They were the Altar Guild, given the responsibility of preparing the church each week for services. Each woman had a month where they were responsible for preparing the communion ware, some light dusting, and getting the flowers for the sanctuary. Luckily, the florist was right across the street—such an easy job! At certain times during the church year, a few would get together and change the paraments and banners in the church. Depending on the holiday or time of the year, there were certain colors that were used: light blue for Advent; purple for Lent; red for confirmation, Pentecost, and Reformation; white for Christmas and Easter and the occasional saint.

Paula Evans

As Lutherans, we didn't worship the saints as the Catholics do, but if a certain saint's day falls on a Sunday, then we change to white. This engendered quite a discussion one June when John the Baptist day was on a Sunday. Who knew he got white paraments? *Who knew he had a day?*

I always chose a summer month because those six months of the church year require green paraments, so there are no big changes. Unless it's John the Baptist Day. Again, simple enough.

How I got to be a member of the Altar Guild is still a matter of debate. I know what I did—I made the mistake of climbing a ladder in front of several eighty-year-old women to hang a banner one holiday. They couldn't manage it with the long poles they used, so just using common sense and taking advantage of the obvious, I placed the ladder and up I went. When I came down, they were all smiling. I couldn't figure out why—I didn't do anything that spectacular.

Except climb a ladder. They could no longer do so safely, and they were in awe of me.

Once again, I'm just too stupid for my own good.

And right then and there, at the base of that ladder, I became the newest and youngest member of the St. Mary of Bethany Altar Guild.

"You people do realize I know absolutely nothing about Lutherans?" I protested.

"Oh, that's all right," they said sweetly. "We'll help you."

"No, seriously," I said, "I just converted last month. I really don't understand what you people do."

"Oh, that's all right. You'll learn."

Advice For The Lovelorn Pakistani

Shit.

As they say, bad news travels fast. I walked out of the sanctuary and into the recreation hall, a matter of twenty steps max, and was greeted by a woman who congratulated me on becoming a member of Altar Guild. *How on earth did she know this?*

I still wasn't sure who all these people were, but I politely thanked her and again stated my misgivings. She patted my arm and said, "Oh, that's all right, honey. Just do everything Doris says and nobody gets hurt."

Hmm . . . which one was Doris? There was a very tall woman who was in charge of something there. Everyone steered clear of her. Yeah, she could kick my ass. But for some reason I thought Doris was literally the "little old lady." She was only four foot, eight inches tall. At eighty-seven, she acted like she was forty-seven.

That Doris? Just do what she says and nobody gets hurt? Naw, it couldn't be.

As the one woman walked away, two of the women who had witnessed the Miracle of the Ladder came toward me, concerned by the look on my face. "Is everything okay?" the taller of the two asked.

I relayed the conversation to them. "She was congratulating me."

"She who?" asked the thinner of the two ever so sweetly, standing just behind the taller one.

I shrugged my shoulders and pointed in a general direction. "Lucille?" asked her friend.

I gave a slight nod. "Could be. I still don't know everyone. Anyway, I told her that I didn't feel qualified to be on Altar

Guild because I'm new, and she said . . ." (I furrowed my forehead at this, as if that would help me understand the situation better) ". . . 'Just do what Doris says and nobody gets hurt.'"

The two women immediately took a step backward at the mention of Doris' name, their faces growing serious, and nodding in assent, almost terrified of a past memory where they had witnessed The Wrath of Doris, maybe even directed at them specifically.

"Oh, yes, she's right," the taller one said. Her friend was now hiding behind her back, her finger tips gently on her shoulder, nodding vigorously.

Now, which one was Doris?

I did enjoy helping these women with their duties. And by the time I did learn who Doris was—she *was* the little four-foot, eight-inch dynamo—I realized how true those words were. Even the one time she asked the pastor a question, he backed up to get out of her reach. She wasn't violent, but no one was taking any chances, it seems. She was very particular and took this Altar Guild job to heart. But it wasn't a power grab or vindictiveness. She truly was doing this to please the Lord.

And woe unto those who would get in her way.

But the Altar Guild is a very nice group of women, the majority of whom are in their mid-eighties. I want to be them when I grow up. They're still active, mentally alert, and just really enjoy life. They go to concerts and plays and lunch all over the place. They're a lovely group of friends. I sit home alone. I know this is my problem and I'm the only one who can undo it or fix it. But . . . I don't know if I want to fix it or if I would even know how to do so.

Advice For The Lovelorn Pakistani

I've kind of gotten used to the solitude. In a way it's kind of nice, but in many ways it's frustrating and lonely. I've never been one for small talk, so being alone is perfect. No one is interested in anything I have to say, or if they are, they are very needy people and want someone to take care of them, more emotionally than physically.

Newsflash: I'm needy, too. I would like for someone to take care of me as well. I don't mind listening to your problems, but, buddy, I've got a ton of my own.

Chapter 13

Fanta and I were on spring break when she e-mailed and asked me to meet her for lunch. She had begun a job at a local hospital working in the lab, so her hours were erratic. I was teaching during the day, but with school on break I had no real plans. She suggested Chipotle for lunch on Friday.

Sounds great! I responded.

Talk about perfect timing! I had free time, I had a lunch date. What could be better? I went to my wall calendar to record this momentous event: *Lunch w/Fanta, noon, Chipotle.*

Then I saw it.

Good Friday.

That's why I was off this week—it is Holy Week. The school has its spring break the same week as Holy Week. But this wasn't the problem.

About the closest my family came to religion was to not eat meat on Good Friday.

I am a carnivore.

Chipotle serves tacos. With meat. Succulent, delicious, cow- and pig-flavored flesh.

This is going to be ugly.

Advice For The Lovelorn Pakistani

I am not much for beans, and the thought of a taco without meat was foreign to me. I've heard of fish tacos, but . . . to paraphrase Ben Franklin: God gave us cows so we could be happy. But my great-grandmother had drilled it into everyone's head, which was dutifully passed down through the succeeding generations, that "thou shalt not eat meat on Good Friday."

I had worked with Catholics for a few years. An early job I had was in the next town south, which we were excited about. It had what was locally known as "Restaurant Row." We were by the shopping mall with all of the restaurants located on the two streets near our building. This really isn't significant, but on Fridays, since our management left earlier, Friday became our "lunch out" day. We would place a group order, and someone would go pick it up for us. It was wonderful until the first Lent. Then, suddenly, it seemed *everybody* was Catholic. They don't eat meat on Fridays during Lent. (And there was Boo-Boo, who didn't eat meat at all on Fridays because he was an uber Catholic. Or an orthodox Catholic. What do you call the Catholics that reject Vatican II and go to Latin Mass? He was one of those. But he's a whole other category.) And, since most of my co-workers were men, they didn't eat vegetables, i.e. no salads. It took us two years to realize that Olive Garden served pasta without meat as an option.

But I digress.

And, yes, I was the one who would get the big-ass roast beef on Fridays during Lent—the one you could smell throughout the building when you walked into the back door. God, those were good. And it was a staple of our staff's diet, except during Lent. And I wonder why I have no friends. Again, I digress.

But this meeting with Fanta was different. I had only been to Chipotle once before—*were there other non-meat options that I could eat?* I mean, other than beans. This was my first Lenten season as a Lutheran, having converted just the summer before. The little they talked about Lent I didn't get the impression that they observed Lent the way the Catholics did. No one mentioned giving anything up for Lent. I didn't get it—Lent or Lutheranism—but it was a glimmer of hope for me. If they didn't give up anything for Lent, maybe they didn't observe the meatless part either. After all, great-grandma died before Vatican II—maybe things have changed?

I can only hope. I did the only thing I could think of—I e-mailed my pastor.

Message line: "Emergency question".

I could just imagine the expression on his face when he received this. He would say half aloud, "Emergency question?" heave a sigh, and, seeing it was a question from me, physically brace himself, planting both feet firmly on the ground. I know this because I saw this reaction all last summer when we were studying Luther's Small Catechism during the classes I took before converting to Lutheranism. Granted, I was the only one asking questions in this class, but mostly because I wanted to understand what they were doing.

I thought I was imagining it, the physical bracing, but I wasn't. I know this because months later I asked him a question while he was standing up and he physically braced himself before agreeing to listen to my query.

This incident also reminds me of my freshman year of college and the mandatory Theology 5 course every student was required to take. The university is Lutheran affiliated, so religion is important. The title of the course was "Introduction to Christianity."

It is more properly called "History of Christianity according to Martin Luther," but I didn't know it at the time. I found this out the hard way. When we got to the second unit of the semester, it was about the Bible. So, for fun, our professor (who was a Lutheran minister) suggested we recite the books of the Old Testament as a class.

He skipped Leviticus.

The class was dutifully, if not dully, reciting the books. We got to about Ruth in the list and I realized I was the only one speaking. The professor was looking at me, a little astonished that I was the only one in the class able to do this simple task.

Now, I learned the books of the Bible when I was about nine. I was going to a Baptist church (we weren't Baptist, but they had a bus service and it got me out of the house and my mother didn't have to do anything, so it was a win-win for her). We were told that we would win a prize if we could recite all the books of the Bible (Old and New Testament). I finally got them down and got up to recite the sixty-six of them. The prize was a pen. It had an orange plastic cover. I was disappointed—a prize means something "good." I can get pens anywhere. *Crap—I was jaded before I even hit double digits. This might explain some aspects of my life.*

Anyway, we (and by we, I mean me and the professor) got to the end of the Old Testament recitation of books and he was astonished and a little perturbed. He asked my classmates, "Didn't you learn this in your confirmation classes?"

Many heads nodded solemnly, a few people a little resentful that they were actually to know this trivia. I had no idea what he was talking about. *What's a confirmation class?* I shook my head no.

He noticed the expression on my face and my response. "Where did you learn them?"

I shrugged my shoulders. "Sunday School?" It was more of a question than a statement. I mean, where else would people learn things about the Bible?

He sucked in his next breath. I wasn't sure what was wrong, but I knew the jig was up. They had been infiltrated by a non-Lutheran. *Shit, what do we do now??*

He mumbled some sort of disclaimer in the form of an apology. I tried to be extra attentive during the class, hoping he would forget that I was an outsider. As we went on, that's when I discovered the class, "Introduction to Christianity" really was more of an "Introduction to Christianity as decreed by Martin Luther." The time came when I had a question because I had no friggin' clue what he was talking about.

He called on me, but gave a disclaimer before he answered: "This is what Lutherans believe."

"That's fine," I replied. "I just need you to explain that again because I don't understand it."

He did explain, I still didn't get it. He tried again. I still didn't get it. After the third time, I just smiled and nodded that I understood, but we both knew I didn't. I don't even remember what it was. I didn't understand it, or them Lutherans. And now, twenty years later, I have become one of them.

Chapter 14

Now that the "carnivore" coast was clear (pastor's e-mail said it was okay to eat meat on Good Friday!), I met Fanta for lunch at Chipotle.

After we exchanged greetings and briefly perused the menu while standing in line to place our order, we were casually discussing what we were going to be ordering. Innocuous enough, but at that moment I didn't realize that eating meat on Good Friday was the least of my sins for this hour.

Fanta was going to order the burrito bowl with the black beans. I admit I have not ever eaten black beans, at least knowingly, but like any three-year-old I kind of wrinkled my nose and, looking even harder at the burrito bowl choices, I mused aloud why none of the choices had meat. As healthy as black beans in reality are, I decided to stick with my usual three tacos with carnitas!

She blanched at that statement. It wasn't until after I had placed my order that I discovered Fanta was a vegetarian. Most Muslims don't eat animals because they are a creation of God.

Somewhere, my great-grandmother is shaking a finger at me, but smiling. *See? I told you no meat on Good Friday!*

Thinking back, Fanta and I had met a few times for a meal. Once at a Chinese restaurant, once at Olive Garden (she ordered eggplant parmesan—I remember this because I had never seen it before, let alone knew anyone who actually ate it). I just thought she was a healthy eater.

Damn, what else could go wrong?

I was about to find out. Obviously, my education from reading *The Secret* took a while to sink in.

We sat at a tall table with the tall chairs that had the rung about halfway up so people could rest their feet on it. Fanta was excited for the company because her parents were in Pakistan.

"Is everything okay with your brother?" I asked.

"Eh, he's all right. They're arranging my marriage." Fanta uncovered her burrito bowl. She shoved it toward me. "Are those garbanzo beans?"

"Wait. What?"

"Are these garbanzo beans?" She poked her fork at the small, tannish-yellow bulbs in her bowl as if her fork was a stick and she was poking a carcass of road kill.

"I think so," I said. *Did she say her parents were in Pakistan arranging her marriage?* "Why? Don't you like them?" I said, referring to the beans, not her parents.

She wrinkled her nose. "Not really."

"So, take it back."

"No, it's okay. I can eat them," she said slowly and mournfully, looking at her meal.

"If you don't like it, take it back. Is it part of the meal?"

"No."

"Did you ask for them?"

She looked up at me. "No."

"So, take it back. Complain. They screwed up your order."

This exchange continued for at least three rounds. I think it was somewhere during the fourth round, I told her, "Just eat it then," and, like a proper three-year-old, she started to whine a little.

"Either eat it or take it back. Your choice."

She looked up at me, almost like she was having an epiphany. "I can really do that?"

"Yes. Just politely tell them this isn't what you ordered, and you don't like garbanzo beans."

She didn't seem too sure of my advice, but she slipped down off her chair and went back to the counter. I turned my head to watch her go. Holy crap—look at that line. Looks like we got here in the nick of time.

Out of the corner of my eye I saw something. I turned my gaze toward the left, and someone was waving. I looked around.

They were waving at me.

I smiled and gave a faint wave back.

Who the hell is that woman? Why is she waving at me?

She left her table and came toward me. *Shit.* We exchanged pleasantries and I tried to rack my brain for clues to her identity. After years of teaching, you become used to former students dropping by to chat, and it may be years between this exact moment and when they last sat in your classroom. So, basically, you lie and pretend to remember who on earth they are.

But this wasn't a student. I don't have much of a social repertoire. I just go to work and church.

That's it! She's from church.
I think.

She and her husband were meeting another couple there for lunch as well. The men were now approaching their table with trays of food, so she excused herself. I smiled at the husband and waved. He gave a faint smile and a limp wave back. *He has no idea who I am either.* I could see his wife quickly explain, more to their friends, who I was, and the sudden realization on the husband's part. Thank God I'm not alone on this one.

Fanta returned, smiling. She had what she wanted. She hoisted herself up into her chair. For some reason I looked back at my church friends. A very brief, albeit startled look crossed their eyes.

How do I explain my Muslim friend? Do I need to explain my Muslim friend? As Christians, aren't we supposed to love everybody?

I turned back toward Fanta, ready to eat. I probably would have already started eating while she was gone except I was distracted by the lady from church. And then again—*am I supposed to wait for my meal partner before I begin to eat? What's the rule? You don't begin eating until everyone is served? But that's at a dinner party and she had been served. But since this meal is an affront to my dining partner, should I have devoured it so she was not exposed to my carnivorous cruelty? But then I'd be staring at her eating, and it's impolite to eat in front of other people. But what if they've eaten their share . . .*

Where the hell do these rules come from??

I tried to go back to where we were, conversation-wise, a full two minutes before. I had no clue what we were talking about. Dammit, think. Think. Think. Something about Pakistan . . .

Advice For The Lovelorn Pakistani

Ah! Her parents were in Pakistan . . .
ARRANGING HER MARRIAGE.
Yeah, that was it.
How the hell could I forget something like that??
"So," I began, "you said your parents are in Pakistan?"
"Yes," Fanta said. She was poking at the contents of her bowl, several times, as if she were trying to find the exact morsel to put in her mouth. "They flew there on Tuesday. They're preparing for my engagement party." *Pokepokepoke.*

I furrowed my brow. "Shouldn't you be there?"
"For what?" She popped her fork into her mouth.
"Your engagement. Aren't you supposed to be there? You're the one getting engaged."
Pokepokepoke. "No, my parents will handle all of that and tell me what happens." *Bite.*

She was very matter-of-fact about this. Again, I know very little about relationships and the quaint little rituals like weddings and engagements. But from what I've heard and seen on TV, it's usually a big deal to get engaged. Usually it's a surprise to the girl. A very elaborate surprise, but she's there to get the ring. And then there's engagement photos that must be taken (which seems ironic as newspapers rarely run them anymore), plus a party and God knows what else.

And Fanta isn't even there? *Did she say her parents would let her know what happened?*

Again, I am learning from my student.

In Muslim tradition, the parents arrange the marriage. The parents make the decision about the spouse, the dowry, the dates. The parents would accept or reject the proposal, it was

Fanta's duty to obey. Communication between the couple was prohibited, but with cell phones and the internet, they would chat. They just couldn't physically be in the same room until after their marriage.

Fanta had photos on her cell phone, which she shared with me. There was one of her parents sitting on a couch. One of her aunt and uncle, who were parents of the groom. Then one of her father and uncle. More photos of the groom between his parents, her parents, and with his siblings.

What could I say? He looked like he was twelve; Fanta says he was twenty-one, the same age as her.

The actual ceremony would take place Sunday.

"Sunday?" I said. "You'll be engaged on Easter?"

Fanta looked at me, not quite sure what Easter had to do with anything. Then it dawned on me. I celebrate Easter, Fanta does not. To Fanta, it was Sunday.

I tried not to sound like a total idiot. "So, now how long until the wedding?"

Pokepokepoke. I was long done with my tacos. She had barely eaten any of her burrito bowl. *Probably because she was pulverizing it with her fork.* "December twenty-fifth."

"Christmas?"

Fanta shrugged. Muslims don't celebrate Christian holidays. I keep forgetting to whom I'm talking. "I guess. My family will wait until the end of next semester when I can go and spend some time there. This summer I am taking classes so I can finish my studies by next year."

"You're getting married but not staying there? Is he coming with?"

Advice For The Lovelorn Pakistani

Well, no, she explained. He has a job and needs to earn money. She has classes to take and a degree to finish. In a few years, when he gets his visa—

A few years?

—he'll move to America and they'll begin their life together. There was plenty of time.

Why, yes, my head *is* ready to explode. This most certainly is one for the books. I just couldn't fully comprehend (translated: over think) the symbolism here, especially when there isn't any. Here I am, Jane Smith, eating meat on Good Friday with a vegetarian Muslim who's getting engaged on Easter Sunday for a Christmas Day wedding. Did I leave anything out?

What an education I am receiving. I don't know why this is such a revelation to me. To Fanta, December 25 is a very practical day to marry. Based on the GNU U calendar, finals week ended on December 19. The family would make the twenty-four-hour flight to Pakistan beginning on December 20, arriving December 21. There are preparations to be made, and meals and rituals for Fanta to observe, so the first available day for her is December 25. It's just practical.

And if you think about it, the dates for the Christian holy days aren't really Christian dates. Easter is based on the Jewish calendar, Christmas is basically usurping the pagan solstice date of December 21.

This is one of those "Only in America" stories. As American as Fanta was in her thinking (very practical and more of a capitalist), she was happy living according to the "old" ways, the traditions that have defined generation after generation of Muslim women. It was almost a sacred duty, proscribed by Allah.

Would we all hold fast to something decreed by our God. What an anchor to have in your life. It gives a sense of purpose I find I am lacking. A grounding that I desperately want. A *raison d'être*, if you will.

But can I handle (or accept) that much commitment? That almost sounds like marriage . . .

Chapter 15

A few weeks later, near the end of the spring semester, Anita called. It was a beautiful day, her final exams were over (as were mine) and her son Don was camping with friends, her daughter was at a friend's party and sleepover, her husband Fritz was traveling on business, and this Sunday afternoon was stretching easily in front of her. She wanted to do something with someone, but she didn't have much money.

Preaching to the choir, honey.

Once again I was beginning my annual "I am going to exercise and lose weight" stint, which usually lasted two days. But it was such a nice day and she wanted to go for a walk, and that sounded like a wonderful idea. I even wanted to go for a walk.

"Come to my house, I have a very little park near my house I like to walk in. We can walk there and talk. It'll be fun."

Sounded like fun. What could possibly go wrong?

And why do I keep asking myself this question? I know I'll be answered, in spades.

I drove to her home, which was about forty-five miles away. It was a beautiful, two-story home in a fairly new subdivision. It had soaring arched windows and hardwood floors. It was really almost too big for the four of them, but then again Anita and Fritz helped me move into a three-bedroom home of my own and there was only one of me. She was finishing washing her dishes by hand, and quickly wiped down the kitchen. She is such a bundle of energy and everything in her home is always immaculate. *Does she ever sit back and just enjoy the beauty?*

Once she was ready, she grabbed her car keys. "I'll drive," she offered.

Hmm, a little neighborhood park you have to drive to? Well, I know people will drive to a walking/hiking trail, so maybe that's what this was. I wasn't as familiar with this part of her town, so what do I know?

I knew we were heading north. Far north. After about fifteen minutes of driving, I began to get suspicious. I saw the signs, but I couldn't believe it. Lake Michigan???

That little neighborhood park was the Indiana Dunes National Lakeshore.

That explained why we needed to drive to get to this "little neighborhood park." It wasn't exactly in the neighborhood. And technically she didn't exactly say "neighborhood," just that it was near her home.

Po-tay-toe, po-tah-toe.

Anita said she and Fritz would take a certain path and then walk along the beach. It was so beautiful, she said. As she showed the gate attendant the annual pass for entering this national park, she handed me a map of the trails. "We usually take number nine. We really like it. It is so beautiful."

She scampered along in her flip-flops as we followed that trail—"It's only five miles!" she explained.

"That had better be round-trip total," I said, trying not to panic.

"Oh, yah, yah, total."

Somehow, I couldn't believe her.

It really wasn't a bad trail. Fairly flat and in some spots even paved. Then, there it was.

The Matterhorn of sand dunes.

And it wasn't even Mount Baldy. Or Mount Tom. Just your regular ol' sand dune. I looked up. I swear this thing touched the sky. I couldn't even see the top of the dune.

Now, I don't move fast. Never did. I told her to go on ahead and I'd be up there eventually. I think it helped that I had been watching *The Biggest Loser*, because the most recent episode was where the contestants were running a marathon. Or was it a 5K? Same difference to me. But they kept emphasizing putting one foot in front of the other, so that became my mantra.

For some reason I knew I could do this. A rite of passage in college was the infamous freshman orientation trip to the Dunes (mockingly called "Dunes Day," a play on Doomsday, because, well, it really was). Later that semester our science class also went there. Mount Baldy was involved both times. The buses were always parked behind Mount Baldy, and if you wanted to take the bus back to campus, you had to climb the dune.

I did it then, I could do it now.

The fact that it was twenty-five years and one hundred pounds ago—I couldn't let those thoughts into my brain.

It took me about twenty-five minutes, but I did make it to the top. Anita was frantically trying to get a signal on her cell phone. *Why?*

"Oh, I wanted to let Fritz know where we are. We love the view from here."

It was a gorgeous view. But from the frantic look on Anita's face, I think she thought I might need an ambulance. *Okay, I'm a little out of shape. Okay, I'm a lot out of shape. I admit it. Okay? And, no, I don't need an ambulance. A hearse, maybe, but no ambulance.*

Little neighborhood park, my ass.

By the time we began the ride home, my breathing was back to normal and my face was more of a cardinal red flush, as opposed to the shade of octopus purple it was when I climbed that Matterhorn of sand. As we were catching up on things, I decided to tell her about Sophia's gift to me, the book *The Secret*.

Anita, it turns out, was into metaphysics. She didn't exactly believe the information about *The Secret*, but she did believe in the power of thought.

She was convinced that the dead communicated with her.

"What?" I asked.

She explained two instances that, if not true, were pretty darn suspicious. One involved her grandmother. She had a vision one night about living next door to her grandmother, in Brazil, and Grandma was floating through the fence to return home. When Anita called her parents in Brazil later that day, she was told her grandmother died the previous night.

A second instance involved a person she had never really met. He was a contractor in Iraq, post-9/11, who had been kidnapped. She happened to meet a relative of his who lived in town. One night, Anita was dreaming and the two had a conversation. "But the odd thing, Smith," she confided, "was

Advice For The Lovelorn Pakistani

he was behind a curtain-like cloud—he wasn't very clear. What do you think that means?"

"That he's not dead?" I offered.

"It could be, but I don't think so. I've never dreamt about him before. And I've never had another one since."

"How long ago was this dream?"

She thought. "Ah, about a year ago. Last June."

This was now the following May and there had been no official word on the fate of this man, one way or the other. Anita continued telling me about how she communicates with the dead, and reincarnation, and quantum physics.

"I really don't believe in reincarnation," I said, hoping to change the subject. *Quantum physics? This involves math, doesn't it? Why am I starting to hyperventilate? Will there be a quiz?*

"Oh, but this book isn't totally about that. It's by a very famous author. It makes you think."

"What book?"

"It's by Edward Cache."

Edward Cash? "Never heard of him."

She looked puzzled. "He's very famous. How could you have never heard of him?"

She glanced at me while she drove. I had no idea who she was speaking about. But then again, with her accent, it could be anybody. But I was usually pretty good about deciphering her speech.

"Spell it."

"What?" she asked.

"Spell the last name."

"C-A-Y-C-E."

"Oh, you mean Edgar Cayce," pronouncing it correctly as "Casey." "Him I've heard of, but I've never read any of his books."

"Oh, you need to. I think you will enjoy them. It's not just about reincarnation. He's very religious."

When we returned to her home, she would take me upstairs to a room they had turned into a library. She had thought of two other books I should read first, to help prepare me for this endeavor.

"You do know I read about a total of two books a year, don't you? When do you expect these back?" I asked her as we pulled into her driveway. As an English professor, especially of composition, you didn't read more than you had to, and you always read with a red pen in your hand—a force of habit. And I always found errors in books. It drives me insane.

Anita laughed, as she unlocked her front door. We headed upstairs to her den, where all of the family's books were shelved. She never looked back at me, solely focusing on her mission. As soon as she entered the room, she dropped her purse and went straight to the shelves. "Oh, you read faster than that. You return them when you're finished." She was up and down, crouching and standing on tip-toes, trying to find the book.

"What's the title of the book?"

"Something about reincarnation. I don't remember exactly." She continued her search.

"Well," I tried to help, "how do you have the books organized?"

"I don't," she groaned. "My son decided to reorganize my books one day last summer. By color. I could have killed him."

Advice For The Lovelorn Pakistani

I took a second look at the book case—it really was organized by color. Kind of pretty, actually. "How did you keep from killing him?"

"I almost didn't. I was so furious with him. Then Fritz told me, 'Aww, don't be so mean. He spent all day working on this.' Yah, but it wasn't HIS books. I think it had a blue cover."

Down she went again and finally found it. "Okay, here's one. Read this one first, but not the very first."

Getting her bearings, she was plucking book after book off the shelf and passing them back to me.

"I'm serious," I said. "I really don't read a lot of books."

"Oh, these are easy reads. You'll get through one a day."

I laughed. "Wanna bet?"

It took me nearly a year, but I did get all six of them read.

Chapter 16

As luck would have it, Frank called me again, agitated. He really hated his wife's boss, Benji. Really, really hated him. He denied it, but he couldn't bitch enough about him. But Frank doesn't "bitch," because that's a naughty word. And he doesn't "hate" Benji.

"Let's just say I'm not his biggest fan," he told me.

Po-tay-toe, Po-tah-toe, I thought.

His wife's employer was having an event to celebrate the success of the China trip. It was a huge project and Shirley played a huge part in the completion of the project.

"Who's Shirley?" I asked.

"My wife," Frank said, slightly perturbed.

Well, excuse me. You've never ever *mentioned her name before.*

But Frank was not one to boast and neither was Shirley. Frank told me so himself. *(I really need to meet this woman sometime.)* But Frank didn't feel she was getting enough recognition.

What? Let me get this straight—neither of you boast about anything. You basically have no ego, but the ego isn't being stroked enough? What am I missing here? Isn't this why there was a celebration—to celebrate the completion and success of the trip?

Advice For The Lovelorn Pakistani

Well, technically, yes, Frank explained. But it coincided with an office-wide party and Shirley was really the star of the night, but she is too modest to say anything and Benji wouldn't bother to notice because he was too busy clawing his way up the corporate ladder. I could hear Frank gasp for air. He was really worked up.

So . . . why am I involved?

"What do I do?" Frank finally asked.

WTF. Someone I've never met is not being recognized for a project I know nothing about, from a boss whom I don't know, other than Frank doesn't like him. She's the star, but not one to brag. And you're expecting me to give you advice to rectify this. Sure—just let me pull something out of my ass for you right now. Don't you have any simple questions I can answer—like what's the square root of Pi??

"Well," my mind was reeling. "Why don't you give her flowers?"

"Flowers?" He'd never heard of such a thing. *How long has he been married?*

"Yes, flowers. If you don't think she'll be properly recognized, you can show her that *you* know how hard she worked. You appreciate what she did even if Benji doesn't."

"Flowers? You mean present them during the event?"

"Not necessarily. You could do it after the event."

"How could I do that? She'll see them."

Jesus, do I have to friggin' think of everything here???

"What about your car trunk? Would she have a reason to go in there? Just put a bouquet in the trunk," I said.

"Put them in the trunk," he repeated, trying to fully grasp what I was saying. "Wouldn't they freeze?"

I rolled my eyes. "They're not going to be in there that long. It's ten o'clock now. Even if you got them before noon, they probably wouldn't be in there more than twelve hours, max. You can wrap them in a blanket if you're worried."

He was mulling it over, and a thought hit me. "And make sure you get her roses," I insisted.

There was a pause.

"That was my next question," he sheepishly admitted.

Oh, my God. How did he get her to agree to marry him? She must have pursued him. If it were up to him, he'd still be planning their first date.

"Does she have a favorite flower?" I asked.

There was another pause, just long enough for me to inject, "You can't go wrong with roses. Just get some, put them in the trunk, and you'll figure out the best time to give them to her."

What am I saying? Well, he's a college graduate, isn't he? He can't really be THAT stupid, can he? But then again, he is a man. And look at who he's asking for advice.

Chapter 17

Several years after our semester together and a few years after the marriage counseling Christmas vacation, I was at home grading papers one September night when I received an e-mail from Greta. It was a pleasant surprise. I had given my students my e-mail because this was the best and easiest way to contact me. She had remembered it.

She wanted to know if I was teaching this particular semester at Central Heights University. I was not. But I told her I would drive to campus to meet her for coffee. She seemed troubled—she admitted as much—and needed someone to talk to. She trusted me and felt she could confide in me.

As honored as I was, I was also worried. What could be so upsetting that she had no one to confide in? *Was it her husband? Her children? Her health? Her family back in Europe?*

No, they were all fine. It was something else, something that happened in class. We agreed to meet early the following week. She had an hour break between classes and we agreed to meet in the cafeteria.

I was intrigued about this, more from a gossipy perspective and maybe because it would boost my morale *(I'm a better teacher than the guy you have now—nyahnyahnyah)*. I didn't know what courses she was even taking or what she wanted. But I liked Greta—she was a nice lady and it would be nice to meet and chat for a little bit.

By now it had been about six months since I read *The Secret* and since Sophia left for Europe. It was odd that I was finding bits and pieces of the book to be so very true. Some of it was pure malarkey, I felt, but some of the ideas were just dead on. I couldn't escape that. One trick that was mentioned was to plan on finding a good parking space wherever you went. And more often than not—I was finding good parking spaces. Even on this day as I was meeting Greta and had to park in the rock-covered parking lot from that infamous rainy day in my very tight, blue Hush Puppies, I found a good spot.

Greta was in more advanced classes leading toward her degree and licensure to be an elementary school teacher. Our meeting was shortly after the anniversary of the September 11 terror attacks, and on the day of the anniversary, her class watched a video about how a teacher should or could deal with students and families from different ethnic or religious backgrounds than a typical white, Protestant American family. *They made a documentary about my life?* When there was a segment of the film depicting a family that was Middle Eastern, some of her classmates cracked jokes that made Greta uncomfortable. And what was more, she said, the professor not only didn't stop them but also agreed with what was said and made a few comments of his own. That bothered her. It bothered her a lot. That's why she contacted me.

"Do I report him?" she asked.

Advice For The Lovelorn Pakistani

"You could and probably should," I said. One thing I had learned is that there were always at least three sides to every story: her version, his version, and the truth. Everyone will interpret a situation in a different way, even when they experience the same situation. I didn't think she was lying or exaggerating about what happened, but I understood where her classmates and her professor were coming from with the comments. Then I realized I was telling a student—and one from another country, no less—that, basically, Americans can be real assholes.

As we chatted, I began to realize she was feeling and saying and thinking of very similar things, almost the same as I. And I thought she might benefit from reading *The Secret*. I hadn't mentioned this book to many people, because it's a very black-and-white proposition. They either love it or hate it, even without reading it. But I felt she understood.

I began to explain my journey with it. It seemed like we were on very parallel paths, the only difference being I had read this book and she hadn't. She was curious, but swamped with homework, reading, raising her children, etc.

She was extremely skeptical, but she trusted me. To her, my life was in order and she was desperate for some stability in her life. I apparently manifested it for her. I told her the story about focusing on the parking spot. She had errands to run after her class and before her children got home from school, and she was frazzled just thinking about it.

"Just focus on getting the perfect parking space. Focus on finding everything you need quickly. See what happens. What's the worst thing that will happen? You have to walk farther in the parking lot?"

She looked at me, her big, blue eyes more like slits under her droopy lids. Poor thing—she was so exhausted.

"So, just wish for a good parking spot and it will appear? That's all I have to do?" She was speaking a little louder than she usually did, almost as if she were trying to convince herself she was not crazy. "That's the craziest thing I've ever heard."

I nodded. "Yeah, but what does it hurt?"

She couldn't argue with that. *What—you make a wish and it comes true? Don't we all hope for that to happen? Isn't that the mantra from Star Wars—"Use the force, Luke." Same thing. Kind of. Sort of.*

What have you got to lose??

It was time for her to go to her class and I headed home. It felt good to talk to Greta. I didn't realize how much I enjoyed her company. It's like we were kindred spirits. She apparently thought so as well, because she began e-mailing me from time to time. The first time was later that evening, to tell me about her successful shopping trip. She did practice *The Secret*, and did wish for parking spaces. Not every single time, but three times that day, she did get a good spot.

In what seemed like a few weeks later, Greta asked me to meet her for breakfast. It was now May. Her semester was over, but her children were in school for a few more weeks, so she could have some time for herself. We met at a restaurant about midway between our homes. Greta was already seated when I arrived. As soon as I sat in the booth, she shoved a wrapped package toward me. It looked like a book.

"What's this?" I asked, surprised but secretly thrilled. *I love getting presents!*

"It's for you. After our conversation, I thought you would like this." She smiled. Her eyes were shining, no more droopy lids.

My fingers lightly rested on the package. I was afraid to move. "What conversation?"

The smile left her face and she looked as puzzled as I felt. "The one in September."

September? It's May—you mean four months from now? This fall?

"Last September?" she prompted.

Oh—last September? We had a conversation?

"Don't you remember?"

Obviously not. Am I getting Alzheimer's? Why don't I remember this?

She couldn't believe I couldn't remember. "You came to campus and we talked?"

I . Came. To. Campus . . . Oh, yeah, yeah, yeah. The 9/11 professor thingy. Okay—I remember now. So, the gift . . .

"So, what happened with the professor?" I asked. Was this a book he authored?

Now she looked blank. "What professor?"

Now I'm confused again. I raised my hand, as if to make a point, but I had no idea what that point would be. "Tell you what—you tell me your story and then I'll see if it matches mine."

After her day of shopping, employing the tricks of *The Secret* for parking spots, while not a perfect day, her errands did go better than she planned. She began to think there was something to this "stuff," so she bought the book and read it.

Keep in mind she's taking fifteen college credits and raising four kids and reading books for pleasure. I have a cat and can barely read a newspaper in one day.

She felt such a connection to this book that she then researched all of the people quoted in the book (at least the living ones. Jesus and Buddha she already knew about). She liked what she saw and bought their books and read all of those. I noticed she had a large canvas shopping bag on the bench next to her. She was pulling books out one by one.

"Have you read this one?"

She was pulling books so quickly I could barely read the title. But the fact that I don't read many books, I could tell from the cover. "No."

"How about this?"

I tilted my head, squinting my eyes to try to read the title or author. "No."

"Anything by Tony Robbins?" She pulled a handful out of her bag.

"No. He's in *The Secret*?"

"No, but he also does motivational talks and I read some of them online, so I bought his books as well. As I was looking for these other people I saw his stuff as well."

I nodded. *I think I've created a Frankenstein's monster.*

I'm not sure what impressed me more—that she bought so many books, that she could afford to buy so many books, or that she read so many books on top of all her classes and family obligations.

Her gift to me was a copy of a book, written by one of the contributors to *The Secret*, that she also owned (with tabs and highlights—she brought that to breakfast as well) which she thought I would like. And she proceeded to spend the next forty-five minutes, through our meal, showing me pages she had highlighted which she found important and applicable to her.

    Indeed, it is true—from your pupils you'll be taught. And as much as I didn't want to agree with her, I did like the book and found the same things true. This was hard for me—the tables were turned, and I wasn't the one with the answers. She did a damn fine job. I'm proud to have had a part in creating such a fine, future teacher.

Chapter 18

I received a phone call from Anita. It was great to hear her voice. It seemed like it had been ages since we last talked. And it had been. It had been thirteen months.

How on earth did that happen? For someone I considered my best friend, how could I have been out of touch with her for so long? Well, she was working on her MBA, so that was taking some time, but still—thirteen months?

Always matter of fact, she told me of her recent surgeries.
Surgeries?
Yes, for breast cancer. A double mastectomy.
What?
I knew she had had a lumpectomy shortly before she graduated and began her MBA. But recent tests showed some abnormalities and more lumps. This was more preventative that anything.

"So what did they do?" I asked.

There was that awkward moment of silence where I realized I was an idiot and had not been fully following the line of conversation. Probably because I was trying to calculate the last time I had spoken with her.

"They removed both breasts," she said, just slowly enough for me to feel even dumber than I already did.

Yikes. What a lousy friend I am.

"Oh, don't worry. Don was here and helped. And Fritz moved back in—"

"Wait—what? What do you mean he moved back in? Where did he go?"

That's when Anita realized we hadn't spoken in more than a year. "Ah, he rented an apartment a few miles away, near the university. We separated."

I think she heard my jaw hit the ground. *Anita and Fritz separated? They had been married nearly twenty years!*

Anita explained her whirlwind year and figured that's why she hadn't called me either. Things were busy. Fritz had lost his job and went into a depression. Their son was ready to graduate next year and Anita was worried about tuition payments while Fritz decided to begin his own business and open a restaurant. She was furious at him because it was just so impractical. Restaurants rarely succeed and if they do, it wouldn't be in time for their son to go to college. It was foolishness on his part and she told him that, over and over again. He got sick of her constant complaining and moved out.

"Was I wrong to feel that way?" Anita asked.

"I don't think so. I didn't know he even liked to cook."

"Oh, he doesn't. I do all of the cooking."

I blinked. This wasn't making any sense.

"So . . . how—" I began.

"Oh, he expects me to do the cooking as well as keeping the books. But, Smith, what am I going to do? I am carrying a full class load—eighteen credit hours—plus I take my treatments in Chicago. I don't have time to cook for a restaurant."

I smiled in spite of myself. Ever since that first semester with Anita, we had this conversation every semester. Too many credit hours, the classes were much more difficult than the previous semester, she had no idea how she would make it through today let alone the entire semester. And her GPA was scraping the stratosphere. She was a hard worker. A very hard worker. A real dynamo. Fritz, on the other hand, was very laid-back. They complimented each other completely. And after hearing Anita explain the situation, I almost had to side with Fritz—it was a lot of nagging on her part.

But isn't that what the wife is supposed to do?

Or is that a cultural thing? Or American? Man, why do they keep asking me these questions?

Anita really didn't need my advice this time. The situation had evolved and resolved itself. They were even seeing other people.

What?

Note to self—call people at least once a month.

Anita was high-strung, but I attributed that to her culture. Granted my entire experience of dealing with Argentines was listening to the soundtrack of Evita ad nauseum during college, but there was a lot of history and some facts in those lyrics! Despite the fact she was Brazilian didn't matter to me. Same difference—like Illinois and Indiana. Different places but same Midwestern values. So, I figure, the same with South America. But Anita was quick and thorough and energetic beyond belief. She never sat still. Hell, she never sat down.

Advice For The Lovelorn Pakistani

Anita and Fritz reconciled in the spring, after seven months apart. Fritz was offered a job, but in Seattle. Since Anita was still gainfully employed here, they agreed she would stay, put the house up for sale and look for a job there, while Fritz moved west with the kids. They would visit each other when they could. She would fly to Seattle, or he would fly to Chicago.

While Anita was job hunting, she would periodically ask me if, in the event she sold the house before she got a job, she could move in with me.

"Absolutely. My casa es su casa, or whatever you call it."

She looked at me, frowning. She spoke Spanish. And Portugese. And German. English was her fourth language. I don't speak any of those. Well, the English part. I guess I should stick with what I know.

Finally, Fritz and Anita came to a breaking point. That house had to go. Nearly every cent Anita earned went to the mortgage. They just couldn't afford it any more. They decided to try to rent it out. She called me on a Sunday afternoon to tell me their news.

"If we rent it out before I get a job, can I come live with you?"

"Absolutely! You're always welcome."

Four days later, they had a renter. "I'll be there Sunday," she told me.

Yikes—I had three days to prepare. The spare bedroom was large enough and had a huge dresser, which was full of my clothes. Those had to come out.

Hangers of slacks I left in the bathroom so I could wear them whenever would have to go in the closet where they belonged.

Now, I was descended from a long line of slobs. I never met them, but my mother told me stories about my grandmother and great-grandmother and their lack of housekeeping skills. Of all the things she inherited, this had to be it.

I knew Anita was a neat freak. After cooking a meal, she would put the food on the plates and then wash the pots and pans before eating the meal. Not only were those washed, they were dried and put away.

This really was a most perfect living situation. During the summer months, I worked straight 4 to 12s at a local newspaper as a copy editor, and while the days would vary, the hours didn't. She worked straight days, Monday through Friday, 8 a.m. to 5 p.m. We literally never saw each other until the weekend. Even though we were sharing a home, we really had the house to ourselves.

That first Friday after she moved in, she called me at home about 10 a.m. She was lonesome—she hadn't seen me all week.

"We'll see each other tomorrow, you know."

"Yah, but I miss talking to you."

The most unusual thing that week was, I swear to God, the bathroom got cleaner every single time I went in there. I couldn't figure this out—I thought my eyesight was really going to pot. I still don't know how she did it. The same thing in the kitchen—that got cleaner with each usage. Even the turntable in the microwave—it had perpetual water stains on it which I could never remove. Within three days it was sparking clean.

"How the hell did you do that?" I demanded.

"What? I just washed it."

"No, I washed it. I scrubbed it. I put it in the dishwasher even. How did you get those stains off?"

The kitchen sink seemed to be a touchstone of sorts with us. The day she moved in, I was standing at the sink washing dishes and we were talking, and she said, "You wash dishes like a German."

"What?"

"You wash dishes like the Germans. They fill the sink up with soapy water and put them all in there." I had seen her wash dishes, and she always washed each item under running water with a soapy scrub brush.

I returned to the sink, then stopped. *What the hell?* "I am German," I announced.

Who knew this was a cultural thing? It's the way my mother did it, and her mother, and her mother before her. The one who came from Germany.

Another great thing about Anita living with me was that she loved to work in the yard. She wanted to trim the bushes. She found an old pair of shears in the tool bucket and, with my blessings, had a go at one bush. I tried to get her to use the electric hedge trimmers, because I remembered why I stopped using those shears—they needed to be oiled as they tended to stick. Which is why I never trimmed the hedges. Even with the electric trimmers. I'm lazy.

One day the lawn mower died. We went to the hardware store to buy a new one. She insisted we buy some mums so she could plant them. We did that and when we returned home, I told her I was going to change clothes so I could mow the lawn. She said fine, she wanted to trim that one bush before I began.

Now, I don't move the fastest, I admit, but I came inside and just changed my slacks for a pair of jeans. I walked outside into a cartoon landscape.

You know those cartoons where the character takes like five snips and fashions something into a work of art? She had completely trimmed TWO bushes in that span of time. I was dumbfounded by the entire situation.

How does she do this? Where does she get this energy? How lucky am I that she's paying me rent for a room, and then throws in cleaning and yard work services! I need to bottle this!

I need to find more chores for her to do!

But almost as soon as it began, it was ending. During this particular week, my days off were Wednesday and Thursday. Anita came home from work that Thursday evening, very angry. She slammed the door of her SUV and I could see a dark cloud over her. It was almost like a cartoon where the dark cloud with thunderbolts and rain were pouring over the person. I couldn't even fathom what had happened.

"I quit," she more growled than said as she entered the back door.

My eyes widened. *Dare I ask?* "Quit what?"

"My job." Between her accent and her mood, the word was chopped.

"Your job?" I repeated, scarcely believing my ears. She nodded. My eyes widened even more. *To have that courage!* "Really?"

She was speaking so quickly and in such a low voice I was having trouble understanding most of what she was saying, but her supervisor, who wasn't really her supervisor, was planning to transfer her to another facility, about thirty miles away, to do data entry work. The distance would be annoying, but she had traveled that far from her former home to her job and was used to it. But the advantage of living with me was that I was about six miles from her job, versus thirty. It didn't take her too many commutes to realize she was spending too much time in the car. She liked this new set up.

But the problem wasn't the distance. The big problem was doing data entry. To my uneducated ear, I didn't understand. But for a Certified Public Accountant to basically become a clerk to enter information someone else developed, it was a slap in the face. She liked *working*, being active, solving problems. She didn't want to sit behind a desk all day not thinking.

I would. Before I knew it, I heard a voice say, "Are they hiring?"

She brushed away my comment. "Eh, Smith, you wouldn't like this job. Too boring."

"I could use some boring."

She smiled, which kind of hurt my feelings. I was serious. *No students, no homework, no grading—what's not to love?*

We decided to go to dinner to celebrate, I guess, for lack of a better term. She had already spoken with Fritz and he agreed with her. He would fly out on a red-eye Tuesday morning.

What? Fly out to where?

She would be moving out, moving to Seattle to join her husband. Since she was no longer working, there was no need for her to be here. That makes perfect sense. And it would be easier for her to live there, in Seattle, where she wanted to work. If an employer wanted to interview her, it would be easier to schedule when you could drive there rather than trying to catch a flight from Chicago.

I was so happy she would be joining her husband, but sad to see her go. We got along very well (okay, we never saw each other, but still we got along very well) but she had to take this opportunity and it was the only logical step she could take. *And, admit it, Jane, you're just upset because you'll have no one to clean your house or do your yard work.*

Well, yeah, that, too.

Chapter 19

I received an e-mail from Greta one morning. She subscribed to "The Secret: Daily Teachings" and every so often she would forward them to me. This one in particular stopped me in my tracks:

"You are a magnet. When you become a magnet of wealth, you attract wealth. When you become a magnet of health, you attract health. When you become a magnet of love, you attract love. When you become a magnet of joy, you attract joy. You must become the magnet of whatever it is you want, to bring it to you. Magnet comes first—manifestation is second. Manifestation is the effect of the magnet of you."

I sat at my computer for several minutes, thinking about this. What do I attract?

I know I'm happier than I've ever been. I have friends! I belong! I have a church! And my church family accepts me for me. They know the power of forgiveness—God has provided that for us through Jesus. We all screw up, but we're forgiven. It can't get much better than that, can it?

But it does. What else have I attracted this past decade?

Frank.

Somehow, his wife Shirley and I have become friends, which is surprising because Frank doesn't like his personal life and professional life to mix *(hmm, sounds a lot like me, doesn't it?)*. Shirley worships me because I "stand up" to Frank. I really don't, but I don't take him seriously. He's a man. They're fascinating creatures, but I just am not sure I want to own one. So, when one of those creatures decides to "tell me" what to do, I just look at them. I'll question them. Shirley never has, because that isn't how she was raised. There's nothing wrong with it, but it's also not how I was raised. And to be questioned by a woman? That isn't how Frank was raised. You know—Me Man. Me In Charge. Yeah? Well, Me Not Impressed. But Shirley is—with me.

And there's Sophia—how could I have ever gotten this far without her? She is one of those people you can see daily and never become irritated with, and she's also one of those people you can see once every six months and it's like you've never been apart. She is always reading, always ready and wanting to learn more. I just admire her. I could listen to her read the phone book and become so enlightened.

And I have attracted the attractive Anita. Beautiful, smart, exotic Anita. She's a Certified Public Accountant working for a Fortune 100 company. She loves living near Seattle. She gets to travel the world. She and Fritz have since divorced, but she has found someone new. She told me about her new love as soon as she met him—*she wanted my advice!* Isn't that sweet? He's a nice man. They both call regularly—I am part of their family. They value me. She and Fritz are both going to take their citizenship test this year—she is very excited to become an American.

Advice For The Lovelorn Pakistani

And Fanta. Beautiful, respectful, pious Fanta. So disarmingly funny, more so because she isn't trying to be. She's an American in a Pakistani body, only she doesn't realize it. She wants me to explain to her the American Way, but she has a better grasp of it than I do. I feel like a fool—I'm not sure what I'm supposed to be explaining to her because she already understands it. And to tell the truth, I didn't realize "The American Way" was even a concept—one of those things I just took for granted because, being an American, it was always just *there*. Her husband is soon arriving to begin residency in the United States and to begin the path to citizenship. He is a wonderful young man and they will make wonderful parents one day. I look forward to helping him study for his citizenship test. Any excuse for me to watch *1776, n'est-ce pas?*

And dear Greta. My adorable, little Earth Mother-daughter. We are probably the closest of all because she still lives in the Region and because her daughters *insist* she visit me regularly. Her eldest said, "You can't believe the change in her demeanor when she comes back from having coffee with you. She calms down so much—she's almost human again."

Funny, I feel the same way after meeting Greta for coffee. It's hard to believe her children are grown and the youngest two are in high school now.

But while I reflect on the people and experiences I've attracted, I realize that all of these people are more acquaintances as opposed to friends. I wonder what the difference is. To me, a friend is someone you spend a lot of time with—you can just go to their house and sit and chat. You see it on all the old television sitcoms—people come over and have coffee and talk and talk and talk. I don't do that. I don't go to their houses and they don't come to mine. So, are we really friends or just mere acquaintances? An acquaintance, to me, is someone you know, but not very well.

Holy crap—with everything I know about these people, I'd say we are more than mere acquaintances. But it also doesn't explain how or why I became their confidant, their confessor, dispensing marital advice to these lovelorn women.

In truth—Fanta isn't lovelorn, Greta and Anita are. I am as well, if truth be known. Fanta is resigned to her marriage because that is what Allah (and her parents) have decided. She is happy to obey. It's like *Fiddler on the Roof*—the first time Tevye and Golde met was on their wedding day. Their parents told them they would learn to love each other. Fanta can happily live with that.

Huh. So, what do I know? Haven't been in this situation, either.

Fanta never wanted my advice. She just needed a shoulder to lean on.

Now that I think about it, was I even offering anyone advice? Anita . . . Greta . . . Fanta . . . Frank . . . Well, yes to Frank. He is as clueless about marriage as I am. But the girls, women really . . . they knew what to do. They just needed a sounding board. Isn't it amazing how something so simple as lending a sympathetic ear can make so much difference? To these women, it meant the world.

Greta finally gave me a clue one day.

"It's because you represent 'home'. We are 'home', here, in America. You provide stability for us. While we miss our families terribly, we're all living different lives now. We can't go back to what we were; you let us believe that it's okay."

"How?" I'm not sure if I spoke that aloud or just thought it. It didn't make sense to me. They were all living lives. Successful lives. Living the American dream. Here I am, the poor schmuck, who is American born and bred, not living the American dream, not feeling at home, not feeling okay. No husband, no fancy car, no fancy vacations, struggling with just getting through life every single day. Which, I guess, is part of living the American dream in some sick, twisted way.

But in their eyes, I am successful. I am the embodiment of the American Dream. They know they need to work three times as hard to get to the point where I am. I am so terribly humbled by this thought.

It's an indescribable thing. By teaching them composition and critical thinking, I've provided them the tools for analysis and self-reflection. They've learned to think ahead and guess the consequences. Are they also learning to make do with what they have? Are they aware of the struggles they will have to endure, as immigrants, the language "barrier" notwithstanding? Have the hard knocks I've experienced been a benefit to them? It's hard to say.

I was entering a crossroads of my life—my college teaching days were over. The Great Recession of 2008 had affected so many jobs, including mine. While programs were being added and dropped and college teaching was requiring a Ph.D., which I didn't have, I decided to do what I was trained to do—teach high school. As this information went out through both of the university's Alumni newsletters explaining the loss of several professors, my three former students called me, concerned. They wanted to meet for lunch so we could catch up. Anita was back in the Chicago area for a conference and scheduling time with all of them was proving no less complicated than planning the D-Day assault on Omaha Beach. I decided instead of meeting each of them individually, to have lunch with them all together.

While they had never met, they bonded quickly. They had me in common and really, I almost felt like I was intruding on "their" lunch. The conversation flowed easily, with lots of laughter and camaraderie. It was amazing to me at the time, and still is to this day, how easily they communicated with each other. A kindergarten teacher, a Certified Public Accountant, and a nurse practitioner. All from different continents. All from different backgrounds. All sitting here in a restaurant in the middle of the United States. What a great country!

But more amazing to me is how these three women are such a huge part of my life. Me. The social retard. The woman who still doesn't know what she wants to be when she grows up, even though I am nearing fifty. How did we come together? How did I attract these wonderful people?

Obviously, I didn't "attract" them. They were in my classes. No-brainer there—they just happened to take the classes I just happened to be teaching. But we each hit it off almost immediately as soon as we met and became great friends after our respective semesters together were completed. *How?*

I admit, I am fascinated by people from other countries. Not having traveled much, even within the United States, I just want to latch onto people who have lived in places I can just barely imagine existing. These three ladies have seen the things I only dream about and can only see on film. But I got to hear the stories, from them, in their lilted and guttural accents, especially the ones about how they all ended up here, in the U.S., in Indiana. Sometimes it was chance; for Anita it was her husband's job that transferred the family. For Fanta, she had relatives already here. The same for Greta. For me, this was where my family settled four generations ago. No excitement there. Nobody bothered to stray too far from the herd.

I envied these students of mine. Little did I know—they envied me. Even though I never knew my grandparents, or great-grandparents, I could visit their graves. I could point to homes they used to live in. I owned books that they had once owned. I had Christmas decorations on my tree they had put on their own tree. Neither Greta, Anita, or Fanta could do that. (And, okay—admittedly, only Greta envied that part about the Christmas decorations, as her parents still lived in Europe, but much of her grandparents' items were lost during World War II. Anita wasn't big on decorations because it cluttered the house. Fanta wasn't a Christian, so Christmas was more a weird thing *you* people did.)

I still couldn't see what they saw in me. What did I have to offer them? Nothing.

They blinked at my question. To them, the answer was very obvious.

"You give us a sense of home, of belonging," Greta said.

"Yah," Fanta added, "you make us feel as if we belong to this country."

Now I blinked. "But you do," I said.

Anita furrowed her brow and nodded. "Yah, but you don't see us as immigrants. You respect our culture and ask questions. You let us share with you. Other people, they're not interested."

Fanta nodded, her gold-sequined, bright-yellow hajib moving back and forth on her head. She readjusted it. *Pin the damn thing down already!* "Yah, especially for my country, they think we're all terrorists. You ask about our families and our traditions."

I was stunned. I never thought of that. *Seriously, am I the only one curious about other places?* Then I thought of Sophia—the herd mentality. I guess it's not so far-fetched that others would not be interested in other cultures.

"You're like a mother to us," Greta said. The other two nodded vigorously in assent.

Mother? That hurt. Couldn't I be a big sister? Even an aunt?

So, there I had it. My dull, boring, Midwestern lifestyle represented home and hearth to these three fascinating women. One man's trash is another man's treasure, as they say. But more importantly, I realized that I do matter. I, Jane Smith, do make a difference. It may not be a continual feeling, but I have bettered the lives of these three women, and they have bettered mine. We're that much richer for having met each other. And I wouldn't change it for the world. For all of my searching, trying to find a "family," I learned that family is what you choose. With all my searching, I didn't realize I had found it. I created a family of my own with Anita, Greta, and Fanta.

So, my marital relationship advising days were over. My adventures with romance were over. I could be sad it was over or happy that it happened at all. I chose happy, whatever that means.

And it was on a bright summer day about 10 a.m. when my phone rang. It was Greta.

She was frustrated—her children were home from school for the summer and Greta was at her wits' end. Her twelve-year-old daughter has discovered boys. On top of that, puberty was hitting with full force and the middle-schooler was becoming disrespectful. Not just disrespectful by back-talking, but by defying her parents orders to observe a curfew, neighborhood boundaries, whatever the order was, Lily was not obeying it. *What was she to do with her?*

Now, if I thought I was unprepared to act as a marriage counselor due to lack of experience, I am even more so unprepared to act as a parent counselor. I don't like kids (that's probably why I teach . . . at the collegiate level), and other than writing a referral for them when they have violated campus rules, I don't know what to do with them. And this is probably why I don't have any kids of my own. Well, that and lack of a husband. Or sperm donor.

As these thoughts are running through my head, I hear a familiar voice speaking. It's my voice! Giving advice on raising children.

If I didn't know what to do about marriages, I most certainly don't know what to do about raising children.

But that's never stopped me before, now has it?

www.ingramcontent.com/pod-product-compliance
Lightning Source LLC
Chambersburg PA
CBHW020422010526
44118CB00010B/375